Emmanuel

Herbert O'Driscoll

EMMANUEL

Encountering Jesus as Lord

COWLEY PUBLICATIONS

Cambridge ✦ Boston
Massachusetts

International Standard Book Number: 1-56101-059-6
Library of Congress Number: 92-24293

Cover illustration: *Head of Christ* by Rembrandt, Staatliche Museen zu Berlin, is reprinted with permission from Preussischer Kulturbesitz — Gemäldergalerie.

Typesetting by Jay Tee Graphics Ltd.

Library of Congress Cataloguing-in-Publication Data

O'Driscoll, Herbert.
  Emmanuel: encountering Jesus as Lord / Herbert O'Driscoll.
    p. cm.
  ISBN 1-56101-059-6
  1. Jesus Christ—Meditations. I. Title.
BT306.4.036   1992
232—dc20   92-24293

Printed in Canada

Cowley Publications
28 Temple Place
Boston, MA 02111

Contents

Child and Lord

At the absolute heart of Christian faith is the belief that in the child Jesus, born from the womb of his mother Mary, God and humanity were interwoven in a way never before present in the world.

This truth is so unique and sublime that any expression of it in any language falls short. We are left to take refuge in metaphors and images, in stories, poems, music, songs, painting, sculpture, and dance. Some are created by simple folk and some by great artists, and in all we capture something of the glory of this birth, this coming of God among us. However, no human effort can capture the fulness of the mystery.

Knowing that we will be defeated, we have the effrontery to go on trying, knowing also — or hoping — that by our trying we may catch a glimpse of Jesus, and even make it possible for someone else to do so, too.

Who Is Jesus Christ for Me?

In 1944 a very courageous young Christian faced death in a Nazi prison. His name was Dietrich Bonhoeffer. He was a Lutheran pastor who for years had resisted Hitler, becoming heavily involved in an unsuccessful plot on Hitler's life. Because of that involvement Bonhoeffer was condemned to die. His family and friends were desperately hoping that the American army's sweep across southern Germany would reach his prison in time. That hope failed and Bonhoeffer was executed.

In the months before he died he wrote a number of letters. These letters have been collected to form a small book — a classic among Christians. In a letter written to Maria von Wedemeyer, his fiancée, Bonhoeffer expresses his conviction that in the years to come the great question for Christians would be: Who is Jesus Christ for us?

It is a deceptive question. It seems simple, but not when we look at it more closely. Notice the question Bonhoeffer did *not* ask: Who is Jesus Christ? Why are these two questions so different? "Who is Jesus Christ?" can be answered by information: "Who is Jesus Christ for us?" cannot; the only response is commitment. Our culture is fascinated and flooded by information; commitment comes harder.

As western culture changes we are realizing, very late in the day, that our love of information, of amassing it, processing it, and sharing it, allows us to remain outside the thing or person studied. If we can remain outside we need not commit ourselves and our culture is discovering that this lack of commitment can have very undesirable consequences.

This discovery is true whether we are gathering information about the planet or about Our Lord Jesus Christ. Even as I write his name and title I am mingling information and commitment. To write his name "Jesus" is information: to call him "Our Lord" is commitment. For a number of reasons many late twentieth-century Christians are realizing that "information-faith" is not enough; they are seeking "commitment-faith." Our Lord, as the one who refuses to die, who insists on rising again and again in history, is once again calling us to commitment.

In every society and time men and women have had to decide who Jesus is for them. Many have left us rich memories of their experiences which can be immensely enriching. Every Christian possesses two communities. There is the Christian community made up of the faces and voices among whom we worship, pray, and work. But also, if we choose it, we have another community. Donald Allchin of Canterbury has a lovely name for it: he calls it our "community in time." It is composed of all the men and women who in their time have sought Our Lord, wrestled with faith, experienced its journeying, and sometimes left us a record of their experience. Mark, Mary of Magdala, Augustine, Julian, Martin Luther, Hildegarde, Francis, Thomas Aquinas, Teresa of Avila: the list is endless and each of us would have a different one. In fact, when we compare the names which are significant for each of us as a community in time, we can tell a great deal about each other's road to faith in Christ and how we now experience it.

But even when we have explored our community in time, even when we have come to know and to love the voices of those men and women whose Christian pilgrimage speaks to ours, we still need to do one more thing. Each one of us has still to decide how we are to respond to Bonhoeffer's question: each of us must decide who Jesus is for us. Is he to be an attractive and fascinating figure in history, an admirable but rather impractical echo in human memory, or is he a living reality to whom we can commit our lives and from whom we will receive grace and guidance to live our lives?

What do we mean when we use words like "committing our lives to Jesus"? I hesitate to frame an answer because every Christian who has ever acknowledged Jesus as Lord would respond differently. Nevertheless, here is what one Christian, limited to his own time, and society, and experience, says committing one's life to Jesus as the Christ means.

Jesus Christ is Lord of my life because I have come to the conclusion that the way he himself lived out human experience is the ultimate or truest way to do so. While I cannot fully embody his ultimate qualities he, nevertheless, gives me grace to continue to search for and to follow his way. When I fail to do so, as I constantly do, I am assured of his forgiveness but, of course, not freed of his discipline. He is also my Lord because I believe that the love he embodied is a living out in time of an eternal love which lives for ever at the heart of things. Finally — and my response is anything but final because in these few sentences I have only begun to respond gropingly to a blinding mystery — Jesus is Lord or Christ for me because I have come to believe that by his death and resurrection I have been shown a profound truth about the whole of creation: God's last word about creation is not death but resurrection.

Between Us

Almost all of this book was written when I was on a study-sabbatical in Jerusalem at Saint George's College. Each day we would learn more of the tradition we possess as Christians. For most of every day we walked and climbed, and sat and discussed, and listened and learned in the places where others, including Our Lord himself, had walked before us. Every time I sat down to the writing of this book I could almost palpably feel Saint John coming up behind me, looking over my shoulder at my page, and saying in a rather resigned voice, "Don't say I didn't warn you."

The first time he arrived I didn't know what he was talking about. After he had come a few times I decided to risk asking him what he meant. He raised an eyebrow and said, "You have read my gospel, haven't you?" and I hastily assured him that I had, many times, and with much gain. "Then," he said, "you must have read the last paragraph I wrote. If you can't remember it, let me tell you what I said. It is a warning to people like you." He closed his eyes and after a few seconds he quoted, "There are also many other things that Jesus did; if every one of them were written down, I suppose that the world itself could not contain the books that would be written."

He opened his eyes and looked straight at me. "You know why I wrote that at the end of my book?" he asked. I knew he wasn't really asking me, he was asking himself and at the same time determined to tell me. "By the time I finished my book," he said, "all sorts of people were writing about Jesus. There were dozens of books. Some were pretty terrible; I wince to this day when I think of them. But it was obvious even then that there was going to be no end of books about the Lord Jesus. After all, what could you expect? Nothing like him had happened before, nor will it ever happen again, the same way.

I realized this truth the morning Peter and I arrived at that tomb. I was terrified. I didn't know what to expect. Mary had come back, mad with joy, saying that Jesus' body was not in the tomb, that she had met him, and he had called her by name. By the time I got to the tomb I didn't know which would be more terrifying, to find his body or not. How do you write anything about that? Where do you begin and how — in such a way that people won't dismiss you after the first few paragraphs as a lunatic?''

''You did a magnificent job on those first few paragraphs,'' I quickly interjected. ''Thank you,'' he said. ''I don't know how I thought of that idea of the Word having been spoken. I suspect it was the Lord himself who put it in my mind.'' Then, as if catching himself, he said, ''Enough about me. Back to the warning I gave in that last few lines of my gospel. I knew the books would never end: they never have! So why are you writing another book about the Lord Jesus? I go around religious bookshops and theological libraries all the time. I am astonished at the endless shelves of books about him. Here you are adding to the pile? Why?''

I hung my head in embarrassment. I didn't really have an answer, at least not the kind of answer good enough for this conversation. ''I don't really know,'' I said. And then I decided to blurt out my reasons and trust that he would understand. ''The truth,'' I said, ''is now that it's finished I realize that I really wrote it for myself. I suspect it is my effort to write down who the Lord Jesus is for me.''

I felt a very gentle hand on my shoulder, and the saint said, ''That's a very good reason, actually. I felt like that when I started.'' This reply gave me courage so I pressed ahead. ''There are other reasons of course. I don't know how much you know about this side of the world at the end of the second millenium, but in the last few hundred years, millions of people have forgotten what you and the others wrote. Oh, they like to quote pieces on various occasions but they've really forgotten the whole story you and the others told. But something wonderful is happening these days. Millions of people are looking for faith again, and among them people are again looking for Jesus.

The only trouble is that it is so long since we had to write simply about him that we've almost forgotten how. Most books assume their readers know a lot about him already. Most people who preach about Jesus assume the same. So I thought I would write a book that didn't assume that. This little book — I held up the early pages of the manuscript for him — is for people who want to know something about Jesus so they can then have him in their lives and in their world.''

"Do you think it was ever simple?" Saint John said. "I mean what happened in the garden, on the cross, at the tomb, all that?'' "No,'' I said, "it's not simple at all. It's the most profound and mysterious thing I can think of, but what I mean is that there must be some simple, straightforward way of telling about him. After all, he himself put the most mysterious things in such a way that you can tell a child a lot of what he said. "Yes, indeed,'' said John, "you can. I always envied Luke's gift for writing children's stuff as well as adult.'' He looked at me and smiled as if he were sharing a secret.

"Any other reason?'' he said. "For writing the book, I mean?'' By this time I was finding it easier to be with Saint John, and feeling a bit encouraged I said, "Have you ever heard of Form Criticism?'' "Of course,'' he said, "it's absolutely fascinating. Mind you, I have often been amazed at the things I've had to learn from scholars about my own book!'' and he laughed.

"I know what you mean,'' I said, "but we've had a great deal of it, and wonderful and valuable though it is, it has formed the style and thinking of many Christians, especially preachers. The result is that until recently we almost lost the ability to speak about your book and the others in a way that really gripped people. We would analyse your writing to death. We would tell people why this or that verse wasn't in quite the right place, and we would say that this or that was true but not literally true (whatever that means), and that this or that passage was not done by you but by a disciple of yours. By the time we had finished with all this fascinating stuff, nobody was really hungry any more to hear what you said about the Lord.''

Saint John looked pained, then he brightened. "But that's all changing, isn't it?" he asked. "Yes, it certainly is," I said. "We've rediscovered how powerful stories can be, how images communicate so clearly, and how deadening endless analysing and explaining can be."

"Can I tell you one last reason for writing this?" I lifted the manuscript. "I've written it," I said, "because I want Christians to learn again that when asked their beliefs about the Lord Jesus they should always reply with the word 'Yes.' So many begin with ghastly stutterings such as, 'Well, it all depends on. . . .'."

"You mean when one is asked about the really important things," said the saint, "like the incarnation and the crucifixion and the resurrection and the ascension." He caught himself and said, "Dear me. I'm beginning to use that kind of language too! Forgive me!"

"Yes," I said, "that's exactly what I mean. Even if we feel the need to explain HOW we believe those things, we should always begin by making it quite clear THAT we believe them."

I realized that I was beginning to make speeches. Saint John betrayed no impatience however. He said quietly, "I've been looking over your shoulder a lot, you know. I'm glad you did one thing. I'm glad you put a lot of people into the book." "But I learned that from you and the others," I said. He smiled. "Do you know why we all did that in our books? Because men and women and children are why it all happened. The Lord Jesus came so that you and I and everyone might have life. Don't ever forget that." Then he was gone.

Just as he went a strange thing happened. It seemed for a moment that there were others behind him and the room seemed to be absolutely full. I had a strange feeling that somehow I knew them all and that they knew me. It was a funny feeling, like meeting a huge family you knew you had, and you had often been told about, but had never met.

I suspect they know you, too.

The Lake and the Land

The lake of Galilee is a beautiful stretch of water. However, a sudden wind from the coastal hills to the west can make it vicious and dangerous. Towards the north the land rises in a series of terraces, and twenty miles to the west is the town of Nazareth.

In Our Lord's day there were small towns all around the lake which lived largely off its bounty. Magdala was on the western shore, Capernaum on the northern end. Further down the west side Herod had built Tiberias, a gleaming resort named after the emperor. It was along the northern shore that Jesus would often have watched the boats returning in the early morning after the night's fishing. It was here he walked towards two contemporaries and said the timeless words "Follow me." There is a fair amount of evidence to show that if Jesus thought of anywhere as home, it was here.

In that long-ago Galilee lived about three hundred thousand people. Down by the lake, Capernaum had about nine thousand. Most were involved in fishing. Capernaum is the best place to look if we want to see the kind of house Jesus would have known. The first thing that strikes you is how tiny they were. The floors were flags of black basalt, the windows minute. There seem to have been four rooms usually, all around a little central court. It was almost impossible to be private. With sunset, reading and sewing and embroidery were put aside; oil lamps were not much help. After dark, it was eating, drinking, talking, or bed, unless you fished for a living and it was your night shift.

Galilee was mostly fishing and farming, with, of course, tailors and carpenters, bakers and butchers in the towns. The fishermen sent salted fish off north to Ptolemais for export. In the countryside there were smallholders, mostly self-supporting in a basic way. Then came the landowners who traded produce. Finally, there were some large estates. They would often have an educated Greek slave as their steward, the kind of person whom Jesus includes in his parables on more than one occasion. All over the countryside were thousands of hired workers. Below these, rootless and homeless and often exploited, were the estate slaves, most of them Canaanite.

And, as always, there were the merchants and through them trade went in every direction, to markets strengthened by several million Jews outside the country. Grain went from Galilee, olive oil from Samaria, dates from Jericho, balsam and salted fish from the lake, and from Palestine the bitumen or building pitch for which it was famous. It was a busy country, alive and productive; it was also seething with discontent. It was in fact a tinder box waiting only for someone to throw a match.

One of our myths of history is that the important parts of the Roman Empire were in western Europe. The truth is that the richest provinces were in the east. Palestine lay in the middle of these provinces, on a coast sometimes called the Levant.

Syria, including today's Lebanon, was the California of the age, a golden, unreal land where everything seemed to be larger than life. From Syria came oil, wine, fruit, textiles, dyes, jewellery, glass. Antioch was the third city of the empire, cosmopolitan and sophisticated, glittering on the river Orontes. We hear nothing of Antioch in the gospels but it figures very prominently in the book of Acts because thousands of Christians went there when things began to become very unpleasant around Jerusalem within a few years of the crucifixion and resurrection of Our Lord. It was the Christian community in Antioch that sent out the very first missionaries.

Beirut was booming as a port. Tyre, Sidon — we know that Jesus travelled in this area at least once — Ptolemais further north, were all competing for trade. Baalbek stood in the Beka' Valley, its cluster of temples the most awe-inspiring architecture in the Roman world. Beyond that lay Damascus.

Then there was Egypt, so rich and vital that it was deemed the personal possession of the emperor. Its corn fed Rome for a third of every year. Its granite was the stone from which

Roman temples were built. Glass, paper, linen, ivory, spices, silk, all flowed across the Mediterranean in the great, heavily armed galleys.

Linking all this treasure was Palestine. It lay across every trade route in the world of that time, at the centre of a strategic triangle of three powerful cities: Petra, Damascus, Alexandria.

Three roads linked Palestine together, the predecessors of the highways of modern Israel. To the west was the coast road, called for centuries the Way of the Sea. Its disadvantage for travellers was that while you enjoyed the coast on the way south, you had to negotiate the dangers of the steep climb through the Judean hills.

The middle road left Galilee and brought you down through the lovely valley of Jezreel, or Esdraelon. To this day the valley is the corn, fruit, and vegetable basket of the country. From there you climbed into the hills of Samaria, continuing south until you climbed a rise and saw Jerusalem.

The third road left the Galilee highlands, turned east to the Jordan valley and ran south to Jericho. After that you veered west to take the Roman military road for the climb up the escarpment and the east slopes of the Mount of Olives. On this road you were safe only if you travelled in caravan: alone you were in great danger. Jesus used at least two of these roads. On the Samaria road he had a subtle and complex encounter with a fascinating woman which John recalls in detail. On the Jericho road Jesus encountered a courageous and determined man who asked for his eyesight and received it.

In some ways it is a mistake to think of Palestine as a country at all. Under a veneer of unity imposed by the Romans there were deep and long-standing differences. The south, Judea, was always smouldering, resentful, conservative. Samaria had been decimated and raped so often it was almost undefinable. Galilee in the north was a world to itself. It had been Jewish for only a few generations. It had a sense of openness to the world, a gentleness, a graciousness. Hillel, one of Israel's greatest rabbis died there, just about the time Jesus as a boy of ten was exploring the streets of Nazareth ten miles away. "Do not unto others," Hillel used to say, "as you would not have them do to you.'' A young mother may well have passed that on to her son. He may have recited it in the village synagogue. He would live and die and rise again as the timeless embodiment of what Hillel had said.

Light in a Shadowed Time

What did the men and women of the first century think about themselves, about life and death, joy and sorrow, about the meaning of human experience? As with us, there was an immense variety of attitudes.

Judaism existed almost everywhere in the world of that time. It was founded on two things: the absolute conviction that God is One Lord, and the conviction that God is All in All, infinite. The first emerged in the ordeal of the wilderness journey under Moses. The second was discovered in exile in Babylon and expressed in the inspired singing of the prophet Isaiah. To many Romans and Greeks searching for meaning and stability in a crumbling world, Judaism beckoned very strongly.

In the ceaseless search for meaning people had at least six choices. You could believe in the Roman state, in Roman law, Roman legions, the Senate, the Roman way of life, making Rome an absolute for yourself (what was at that time called a god). You could observe the life of the local Jewish synagogue, responding to its high moral demands even though you were not Jewish. You could be initiated into what was called a mystery cult and gain a certain sense of belonging from its close corporate life. You could choose a mixture of cynicism and Zenlike detachment, call yourself a Stoic and commit yourself to a very disciplined lifestyle. You could always wash your hands of the whole thing and go and join a remote community. Finally, you could rage against life in general and join an organization committed to political violence. How familiar all this sounds in the late twentieth century!

Come and walk for a moment along the golden curve of the beach in Caesarea. Today the city is nothing more than a ruin but it is still haunting. It was built by Herod using state-of-the-art engineering, and it stood for the Roman choice, the belief in Roman power, Roman know-how, Roman gods.

In that religion everything had a god: a person, a family, a regiment, a guild; values in life, such as honour, chastity, ambition, love — all had gods. You could take your friend's gods into your life and so bond the friend to you. Wherever the legions marched they brought home more gods to Rome. From Egypt they brought Serapis and Isis, from the Euphrates Ahura Mazda, from Asia Diana. From Greece they brought Cybele and Zeus and Attis and Orpheus and a hundred more. It was, in part, this huge inpouring of gods and sects which was sapping Rome's moral energy. Augustus tried to stop it just about the time Mary gave birth to her child, but it was too late. The flood of cults was a symptom of the insecurity which would eventually become loss of hope and identity.

Men and women of that time wanted desperately to believe that a new world was beginning with Augustus. The truth, however, was that too much had been forgotten, too many priceless treasures had been allowed to rust away, and not just in Rome. At Jesus' birth the greatness of Athens was only a distant memory; Greek tragedy and comedy, once able to express the terror and mystery of life, were in decline. The sense of participating in public affairs — what the Greeks had called democracy — had been trampled by Roman legions. Science, mathematics, and medicine were largely coasting on past achievement. In Jerusalem, Judaism was exhausted and embittered and divided by two centuries of savage struggle for survival in the face of Greek culture. The glorious universal visions of Isaiah were forgotten, and everywhere there was the chill of something lost, and a longing for something unknown.

Into this shadowed time Mary brought her child. She did not think of him as divine redeemer. His baby mouth sucked at her breast, and thirty years later she would hold his adult corpse in her arms. But for some reason he would not die. Pronounced dead by countless voices and movements, he would continue to touch and form human experience, walking the earth on the feet of others, and speaking with other voices. His hands would go on touching humanity through its own hands of mercy and caring. Mysteriously and powerfully he became "Jesus Christ, the same yesterday, today, and forever." And as spring came to Galilee and life came to her womb, Mary sang perhaps the final word: "From henceforth, all generations shall call me blessed."

A Hospitable Man

The gulfs that yawn between the hill village of Bethlehem in the first century and the worshipping congregations in the West in the late twentieth century, almost defy the building of bridges. Moreover, language and cultural assumptions can disguise these gulfs and ensure their existence.

We read that when Mary and Joseph came to Bethlehem there was "no room in the inn." The very phrase has become part of our language as an expression for lack of hospitality. Instead the holy family are given a manger which later centuries understood to be in a stable. The implication is that the family was refused comfort; they were rejected. On this theme countless images have been painted, countless stories told, countless sermons preached, countless scenes in Sunday School pageants played out.

Figuring prominently in this tradition is a simple man who tried his best to carry out the duties of a very difficult and thankless job. We don't know his name; he is not given a single line to speak in the Christian drama; he is not even mentioned in scripture. But the story is hardly ever told without him.

Generations of children and adults are quite certain what he said. For two thousand years this innkeeper has been made to utter his rejecting words in the plays of children and therefore in generations of adult assumptions and imagination. The innkeeper said No; that reply has always been beyond argument.

We should argue about that assumption on behalf of this unknown man. As I write these lines I am sitting on a stone step outside my room in the courtyard of Saint Margaret's Hostel in Nazareth. From the verandah of this quiet, gracious place I can see modern Nazareth spread across the surrounding hills. A little while ago I was being told about of an eastern inn as it would have been south of here in the Judean plateau that long-ago night when Mary and Joseph sought shelter.

The inn was built around a central courtyard, as, for that matter, is the one I am now in. There all similiarity ends. In Jesus' Bethlehem there would have been no rooms as we understand them, no beds, no privacy, no toilet facilities, and no comforts of any kind. All that would have been there was an open area surrounded by a protecting wall with gates open until darkness fell. During the last hours of daylight travellers would occupy spaces on the ground until the last square foot was taken, and in times of feasts and holidays, bodies would have been almost on top of each other. Add the beasts that accompanied travellers and we have some concept of the reality. This was not the place for a young woman in the last stages of pregnancy. Perhaps we may now begin to form a rather different script for the unfortunate employee who has to preside over this weary, cramped, and volatile mass of human beings and animals.

Think now of the manger of Christian tradition. Again the reality is rather different. Bethlehem is built on a ridge of rock, and that ridge is riddled with caves. These caves have always provided human beings with shelter, and to this day they are warm in winter, cool in summer. What is more, these caves and many like them were the earliest chapels of our Christian faith. For the early Christians the cave, far from being a place of rejection, became a place of hospitality, spirituality, home, nurture, security. We think of Mary and Joseph being dismissed from the imagined comforts of an inn, which we tend to think of in our terms of comfort and warmth, and relegated to the bleakness and misery of a manger or cave.

Now try to meet our innkeeper again. He sees a young woman about to give birth within hours. He looks at the heaving mass of humanity and animals behind him. Thinking desperately how he can help, he remembers the security and warmth of the caves below the ridge. He makes his offer, and Joseph may well have blessed the man for his kindness. Ironically, if Joseph did, his is the only blessing the unfortunate man has ever been given!

We are all the innkeeper to whom the Christ comes. The inn of our personal life is almost always desperately overcrowded. Our plans, hopes, fears are beyond number, and too often we justify the closing of the gates of our soul. But if we are prepared to play the innkeeper's part as that long-ago man may well have played it, we may realize that there is always a place of hospitality for the Christ who searches for his birthing in us. The cave therefore is always the forgotten place in us, the rejected place, the unseen place, that part of us dismissed as second class. But the cave is where the Christ is born.

The Cave and the Sword

Around A.D. 130 there was a man named Justin who lived in Nablus, a town about twenty miles north of Bethlehem. He writes: "If anyone desire other proof for the birth of Jesus in Bethlehem, let him consider that a cave is shown where he was born and a manger in the cave." About a hundred years later there was a man named Eusebius who lived on the coast at Caesarea. He writes: "The inhabitants of Bethlehem bear witness to a story that has come down from their fathers. They point to a cave in which the Virgin laid her child." About a century after that, Helena, the mother of the Roman Emperor Constantine read this. Her son had just embraced the new Christian faith, and Helena had his support and all the power and money of empire. She built the Basilica of the Nativity on the side of the hill at Bethlehem, sinking its foundations deep into the hillside where memory had preserved the site where Mary had laid her child.

Within thirty years that child, now a man, would suffer one of the most brutal deaths imaginable. Within another thirty years there would be groups of people in almost every major city of the empire who knew his name and gave him an allegiance which could cost them their lives. In another two hundred and fifty years the empire would acknowledge him as its God and Lord. Today in every society on the planet there are at least some men and women who acknowledge him as the central reality of their lives.

As Mary and Joseph groped their way to wakefulness in the early dawn, exhausted and exhilarated, they could not know that the human story had been for ever changed by the coming of the tiny form for whose life they were now responsible. In the days that followed there were three things that had to be done. The child had to be circumcised; this could be done in the village by the local rabbi. Later, the child should be presented in the Temple. Finally, his mother had to observe the days of her purification. In Jewish law a woman who had given birth had to wait until all the birth fluids had ceased to flow from her body, so that she could be declared pure again by a priest.

To present their newborn child to God the parents came to Jerusalem, most likely using the beast they had brought from Nazareth. Jerualem was one of the great cities of the Roman world, standing above the Kidron Valley on a ridge of rock. Herod the Great had virtually rebuilt it, and above its narrow streets soared the symbols of power. To the south-west stood Herod's own palace; to the south the vast stadium for the games. At the north was the Antonine Tower, built for the Roman garrison, and named after Herod's great friend and patron Mark Antony. Into the city, soaring across the deep valleys, more than seventy miles of stone aquaduct brought the vital supply of water.

The day that Mary and Joseph arrived there would have been about sixty thousand people living in the city. While they were mainly Jews, there would also have been some Roman military and civil servants, Greek actors and teachers and artists, Persian business men, Egyptian professionals of all kinds. Some of the mercenaries in Herod's private army would have been Celts from as far away as the Black Sea. Dominating everything would have been the Temple, still unfinished after nearly forty years of planning and building.

This building was the focal point of the Jewish faith. Jews came here from every part of the known world, bringing the equivalent of the statutory temple tax, half a shekel. That tax made the Temple one of the most powerful financial institutions of that world. Within two decades it would be powerful enough to lend a senior career diplomat named Pontius Pilate so much money that he would become politically and personally compromised. It would also be powerful enough to influence decision making in Rome itself.

The couple may have felt terribly lost as they crossed the great open area of the complex, eight city blocks long. At its highest point it overlooked a one-hundred-and-twenty-foot drop of quarried stone. At its greatest height the sanctuary stood higher than a Gothic cathedral of the Middle Ages. All of it shone white under the sun and sky.

Mary and Joseph bought the cheapest things permissible for a sacrifice, two birds. Their hearts quite naturally overflowed with joy as the priest took their child, made the gestures of dedication, took the birds, swiftly sacrificed them, and handed the baby back. They turned away, but just then an elderly man shuffled from behind a pillar, to be followed by an even older woman. Taking the child into his arms the old man sang a song the parents could only partly understand. He seemed to intuit great significance for their child. This intuition was echoed by the old woman — all very puzzling to the young couple but naturally pleasing. It was only after he returned the child that the old man looked steadily at Mary, then said something she would remember all her life. "Because of this child," the old man said, "a sword shall pierce your heart." Then both he and the woman were gone, and the crowds surged around the young family once again.

The Old King and the Young Child

Because we meet Herod primarily in the pages of the New Testament it is easy to forget that he was a major player in the power struggles that racked the Roman empire, a person history records as Herod the Great. His marriage had brought him the immense financial clout of one of the huge business houses of Petra, the ancient city in the desert which had sat astride the trade routes for centuries and drew vast customs revenue. Herod was not originally a Jew. He was an Idumean from the desert area south-east of Jerusalem. He had appeared at a time when the Roman occupiers were looking for dependable client rulers who would keep the peace for them and collect the taxes which ran the machinery of empire. In Herod, Rome found a capable, even brilliant, politician and tactician who remained faithful to his Roman masters for nearly half a century.

Herod made one great mistake which nearly cost him his career. In the struggle between Octavius and Mark Antony following the assassination of Julius Caesar, Herod supported Antony. When the latter became obsessed with Cleopatra of Egypt — against Herod's impassioned advice — and subsequently lost the power struggle to Octavius, Herod found himself facing a man who now wielded absolute power and was determined to deal with his political foes. In a famous meeting which took place in Cyprus, Herod rescued himself by confronting Octavius and saying to him, ''I want you to consider not whose friend I was, but what kind of a friend I can be.'' Three weeks later Herod and Octavius rode together down the coast road to Joppa and up the hill climb to Jerusalem.

All such triumphs were long over when Mary had her child. By then Herod was seventy years old and extremely sick in mind and body. If Joseph had looked to the south-east as they returned from the Temple in Jerusalem he would have seen the Herodium, the huge fortress which was Herod's summer palace.

Herod was what we would call today a "westernizer." He had always felt that the only future for the Jews was to become Greco-Roman in culture. He was also very much aware that the fires of Jewish nationalism were always ready to ignite. He was constantly on guard for another local firebrand with pretensions to national leadership, claiming to be the Messiah who would remove the Roman oppression. Herod knew well that a single message sent north to Roman headquarters in Syria would bring the Tenth Legion down to Judea with devastating consequences.

Far away to the north-east, in other palaces and temples south of the Caspian Sea, the study of astrology absorbed the energies of Persian intellectuals. In the clear skies of that high plateau they had watched the conjunction of Jupiter and Saturn in the constellation of Pisces. Their charts told them that Jupiter symbolized a ruler, Saturn was the star of Palestine, and Pisces symbolized a time of change. So their journey began: south-west across Mesopotamia, fording the great rivers which gave the area its name.

Eventually they rode up the steep military road from Jericho, then turned south until they reached the guarded entrance to the Herodium. They asked to see the king, and their obvious stature gave them entrance. They rode up the long driveway that circles the mountain to this day. Eventually they came face to face with a dying man, made even more dangerous because of his pain and self-loathing. Courteously they gave the reason for their journey. Then one of them asked the question that was to bring death to a whole generation in the village on the nearby hillside. "Where," said the Persian, with as much nonchalance as the question would allow, "is he that is born King of the Jews?"

Even in his awful state Herod kept a cool head. He went

through the motions of consulting his advisors about local tradition. They pointed to the village he could see from his balcony, the village called Bethlehem. However, no order was given; the iron rules of eastern hospitality held. Only when the Magi were on the point of leaving was the matter referred to again. Herod himself wanted to honour the child they might find, and would be grateful if the visitors would return and direct him to the place.

Only when the days went by and the visitors did not return did Herod act. He had killed before, many times, but never on this scale. The great doors swung open and the death squad rode toward the village. The screams of dying children and of their distraught parents would echo for ever down the centuries.

As the soldiers carried out the slaughter of Bethlehem's children, a family of three, a man and a woman and their newborn child, pushed on as quickly as they could toward the south-west, working their way toward the Egyptian border, probably heading for the million-strong Jewish quarter of Alexandria. There it would be possible for Joseph to get some work. There, too, they would be safe, at least for a while.

Questions and Responses

*As we read the gospel narratives we discover they inter-
sect with our own experiences to an extraordinary degree.
We read of Jesus' confronting someone with an issue and
we realize that the words have leaped off the page into
our hearts. We realize that we face that very issue, or,
as so often happens, have been avoiding it!*

*At the opening of this century Albert Schweitzer was
concerned that people were so busy looking for precise
information about a long-ago Jesus that they failed to realize something all-important. Here are Schweitzer's own
words: "He comes to us as one unknown, as of old he
came by the lakeside to those who knew him not. He
speaks to us the same words — follow thou me. . . . He
commands, and to those who obey him he reveals himself in the toils, the conflicts, and the sufferings which
they shall pass through in his fellowship; and, as an in-
effable mystery, they shall learn in their own experience
who he is."*

The Quest

The question Who is Jesus Christ for us? cannot be answered merely by information. It is, therefore, more than a question, more of a quest. When we find the answer to a question we get on with other things. But to have a quest is to possess the very thing that *allows* our lives to go on, that calls us to follow after it. Jesus Christ is not a question to be answered; rather he is a quest to be lived.

It is very easy to feel that while we have to search for Jesus, the first generation of Christians did not, because they actually knew him. That's partly true. The very first followers of Jesus had the almost unimaginable privilege of living daily life with him. However, they did not see themselves or their daily experiences as we see them. Nobody in the gospel story ever said to him or herself, "I am a character in a story that is going to become universal and eternal!"

We look at them through a two-thousand year religious lens, recognizing the immense significance of their moments with him. We accord endless levels of meaning to those stories, healings, incidents, experiences. But we need to remember that Peter the fisherman and Mary from Magdala and all the others had to spend the rest of their lives working out what those fleeting months of friendship had meant for them. And then they had to work out the meaning of the terrible and mysterious events of the last few days before everything changed and they were all faced with the stupefying fact of the risen Jesus.

We might be tempted to point out that Peter confessed his full faith in Jesus as the Christ in a conversation at Caesarea Philippi. Jesus asked them, "Who do you say I am?" and Peter responded, "You are the Christ, the son of the living God." However, you and I can say things, thinking we understand, but then find that we have to spend the rest of our lives growing into a true understanding of what we said! Two young people stand at an altar and say, "I will love you." They know what they are saying and yet they don't. Then they spend the rest of their lives finding out, and sometimes having to work out, what they meant when they first said those deceptively simple words.

The quest for Jesus is like that, and it is one of the things every Christian, and every Christian community, must do. We may discover Jesus in our childhood, but the images of Jesus from our childhood will not of themselves carry us through the rest of our lives. We grow into an understanding of the cross only if we have had some experience of suffering and failure and limitation. We will never know how Peter really felt when Jesus told him he had to forgive seventy times seven until we ourselves have had to struggle to forgive someone who has hurt us deeply.

The same is true for a Christian community. A congregation may have a struggle with its realization, or sometimes its denial, that Our Lord is calling it to be very different from what it used to be. Once its area may have been pleasant suburb. Now it may be on the way to becoming unpleasant urban! The Christian community or even a whole society may have to quest for a new role to which Our Lord calls it. Some of the churches of Eastern Europe have had to struggle to remain faithful over decades of repression. Quite obviously they have been given grace to find our Lord and to feed on him in that wilderness. Now they have to continue their quest to find his presence and his will for them in a new freedom.

Some Christians feel uncomfortable with the thought that our relationship with Jesus is a quest. A quest hints at doubts, at detours, at painful cul-de-sacs on the way. There are Christians who feel the relationship must always be an intense call. For some there is indeed an intense call, but for others there is no particular blazing moment. But, however our relationship with Jesus has been formed, it will be followed by times of discovery and it will lead on to times of joyful certainty. Always, however, it will demand searching, changing, maturing.

If again we look at a marriage as a pattern, we may find constant commitment and faithfulness. There will certainly be times of intense and joyful mutual presence, but there will also be a continued search for the totality of the other person, a journeying and sometimes even a testing as each partner works at mutual understanding, accepting, forgiving. No relationship stays the same. Every relationship that hopes to be enriched by time has to contain some element of mutual questing. There is a wonderful balance here, in that the warmth and richness of a relationship can itself supply the energy for searching for even greater depth and richness within it.

Likewise Christian faith will give us moments of a deep and reassuring sense of Our Lord's presence. Once again, as with a human relationship, the very richness of our developing relationship with Our Lord will supply the energy for our further questing for his grace and presence. But always there will be the questing. Jesus himself speaks very often in terms of questing and journeying. "Come unto me," he says. Again, "Follow me." At the tomb we are told that "he is gone before you." He asks two people, "What are you seeking?" The quest is for ever.

What Do You Seek?

Sometimes we will hear something indirectly, or overhear it. It will be said to someone else but strangely it will affect us even more than if it had been said to us directly. Søren Kierkegaard writes vividly of overhearing an elderly man talking to a boy in a cemetery. As Kierkegaard passed by he heard the voices on the other side of a wall. The elderly man was comforting the boy. He spoke quietly and intensely of life and death and the hope of an afterlife. He spoke to the boy about his father in such a way as to help the boy to feel pride in his father's life and work. Neither man nor boy ever saw the passerby but he never forgot the power and grace of the old man's words. Kierkegaard used the incident to point to his realization that the conversation was powerful in its effect on him precisely because it was not addressed directly to him. He had not so much heard as overheard.

This way of being addressed can be a very large part of our relationship with the gospel. It is precisely the way that many of the things Jesus said come down to us. We are not so much hearers of the gospels as overhearers. The words will have been said to a man or woman long ago but as we read, they suddenly develop an astonishing power to penetrate our consciousness.

There are at least three questions Jesus asks that have this quality. Each was asked in a particular situation but in each case the question pushes its way out of the particular and becomes universal. Each question seems to be very simple, to be completely and naturally part of the context in which it is asked. So it is; however, as time goes by and the question is asked again and again in scripture, we realize it speaks continually to our human condition. This quality in scripture is exactly what we mean when we say that scripture is a "living word.'' It remains continually alive.

The first of Our Lord's questions is asked in circumstances that are rather sad. In the years before Jesus had begun his public ministry his cousin John had become very well known as a powerful public speaker. John had probably become what was called a Nazirite. He had embraced a way of life that some were choosing as a way to God and a way to find meaning in a changing world. They lived alone in the desert in prayer and contemplation, eating frugally, allowing their hair to grow long. John had returned from the desert convinced that great changes were demanded of individual life and of his whole society: God was bringing in a new age. John's message got a tremendous response. Crowds poured down from Jerusalem to hear him, and many accepted ritual cleansing in the Jordan as a sign of their commitment to a new way of life. Because of this John became known as the Baptizer or the Baptist. We meet John in scripture at a time when Jesus is just about to begin his public ministry, and John's ministry is about to end.

John is talking to two of his disciples, and Jesus passes by. It is John who notices him, and immediately points him out to the other two. It is a very poignant moment because it indicates how fine and secure a person John is. He must know that his life's work has peaked, yet he shows no jealousy or resentment.

The two disciples move away from John and follow Jesus at a distance. After a while Jesus turns and asks them, ''What do you seek?'' Not knowing what they are really looking for, they stammer, ''Where are you staying?'' It is a flimsy, hastily contrived response, but Jesus quietly and easily replies, ''Come and see.'' The encounter was so significant that one of them years later recalls, ''It was about the tenth hour,'' about four o'clock in the afternoon. It is intriguing to wonder if the person could have been John the evangelist who is himself telling us this episode.

What do you seek? is the question of Our Lord that echoes through time. As we come to it in scripture, we need to stop, close the Bible for a while, imagining Our Lord to ask us quietly and piercingly, ''What are you really looking for in life?''

None of us finds it very easy to frame an adequate reply. Certainly there are lots of possible replies, but this is not the same question the genie asks in old tales when it is freed from the bottle. Jesus is not asking for our three favourite wishes. He is asking us to go deep down into ourselves and try to get at what motivates us. It can sometimes be that we don't like what we find, but it can also be true that we begin to come to terms with that newly found knowledge of ourselves, however unwelcome it may be. We can begin the work of changing our motivations and objectives in life. Jesus' question then becomes two things: it is at once an invitation to the turning around of our deepest selves — what the Bible calls repentence — and it can also be an offer of grace whereby our Lord can help that process to begin.

Do You Want to Be Healed?

It is a question that many a doctor has wanted to ask a patient. Probably it would be hard for them to disguise their frustration and even anger, faced with a patient who is showing signs of not actually wanting to be healed. The temptation for the doctor to walk away from the situation must be great.

If we believe that Jesus fully shared our humanity, there is no reason why there would not have been some weariness or exasperation or even anger in his voice when he asked the question. Jesus asked it standing in the noise, smell, and general squalor of a public place in Jerusalem. We must imagine him in a building open at the sides, perhaps roofed — a large public pool, the pool of Bethesda. Around the pool, in every conceivable position and condition, is an appalling cross-section of humanity. Because the waters of the pool have their source in a volcanic spring they become disturbed at intervals. When this happens there is a sudden desperate surging toward the water, a mad rush in which the strongest survive and the weak are pushed aside.

As we look through Jesus' eyes we see one particular man. Every line of his face, every movement of his body, communicates that he has long ago given up hope of benefiting from whatever healing these waters might have to give. The whole point of being in this place is to offer one's body to the mineral springs when they surge up in their white, bubbling froth. When he goes to speak with the man, Jesus learns the appalling fact that the fellow has come and gone from here for thirty-eight years! He has already endured a life sentence in this place, one that probably began in great hope but has now become a pointless vigil, full of sullen anger and, probably, self-loathing. Certainly his outburst in reply to Jesus has undertones of resentment and self-pity.

At this moment Jesus asks his question. Everything we know of Our Lord would suggest that when he was with a person, he was totally present. Looking very intently at the man, deliberately giving him the impression that for this moment he is the only human being in the world, Jesus asks, "Do you want to be healed?"

We hear a question which moves out of that long-ago place of suffering and desperation to any moment and any place where healing is sought and offered. It pinpoints a mysterious aspect of human personality. There are certain conditions in life, in themselves anything but desirable, which in some perverse way we come to find desirable. Consciously, we may believe that we want to be rid of them; we may even say so again and again. However, at a deeper level of our being we have become identified with the condition or situation and we have lost the capacity even to try to move from it. Whether it is an undesirable relationship or physical or mental condition, it is nevertheless familiar. It has become in a deep sense who we are. We have begun to find our identity in it and without it we would not know, or we are afraid we would not know, who we really are.

Perhaps we hate someone, or that there is an old festering resentment. Perhaps it is the kind of illness that has made it possible for us after a long time to manipulate others. This may be what Jesus discerns in the man at the pool of Bethesda. His condition is the means by which he now identifies himself; the pool area is both home and prison, both loved and hated. To change his condition would be to lose identity, to lose his sense of where home is. On the surface he sees himself as victim. He has waited thirty-eight years to get into the pool, but each time others get there before him. In reality his defeats are now probably self-perpetuating; each one only feeds his anger and hopelessness. If left to himself he will forever succeed in what has become his real, unconscious purpose — not to succeed in getting into the pool! To reach the pool would be to risk healing. It would risk ending the kind of world in which he has become at home.

When Jesus asks this man the question Do you want to be healed? he is asking it to each one of us. For us to respond to Jesus with a genuine Yes is to begin the process of our healing.

What Do You Want Me to Do for You?

Once again we are listeners as Jesus addresses someone: what he says is not for us, yet in another sense it is. We are just beyond Jericho, probably slightly south-west of the town. To this day one leaves Jericho with a certain unwillingness. One emerges from its trees and citrus stands, its intimacy and comparative cool, into a world of rock and dust. To the west, half-hidden by heat haze, is the escarpment which forms the side of the valley. Winding snakelike upwards is the old Roman military road, once the most sensible way to go on this dangerous journey because it was patrolled and afforded the best chance of a safe journey. However, as we know from Jesus' choice of this road as a setting for his story about the good Samaritan, such safety was only relative.

It would have been unbearable to walk this steep incline at high noon. It would also have been very important not to get marooned on it after nightfall. We can presume therefore that it was somewhere near the lower end of the road at its first flat stage that the beggars sat. They would not necessarily be beggars in an economic sense. The determined man we now hear shouting for the attention of Jesus was desperate for healing rather than money, although in that society loss of sight would have ensured poverty unless one had amassed a great deal of money.

In those days every public place had its flock of both men and women asking for help, sometimes displaying the most ghastly wounds and sores to win sympathy and support. This man's voice must have carried above the others. It is the disciples who first became aware of him. By now Jesus' reputation has made these pleas a commonplace part of every day. The disciples have probably become adept at picking out the potential nuisance who should be kept away. Moreover, they know this is no ordinary journey for Jesus. His words and his behaviour communicate strain and exhaustion.

At first a couple of them approach the raucous voice and tell him to desist. Being fishermen, it is unlikely they use such a gentle expression! But their efforts have no effect. In fact the only thing they achieve is to make the man shout all the louder. Wisely he realizes he has gained attention. However, the disciples may have become belligerent, and there may have been a scuffle, because Jesus turns, and perhaps with a hint of resignation in his voice, says simply, "Bring him to me."

So Bartimaeus stumbles out of anonymity and stands in front of Jesus. They face each other, Jesus and this ordinary but determined man who will draw from Our Lord's inexhaustible depths of compassion. Jesus looks at him and asks the deceptively simple question: "What do you want me to do for you?" There isn't a moment's hesitation in the reply: "Lord, that I may receive my sight." The words tumble out, overtaking one another in their intensity of hope and longing. And into that intensity and desperation Jesus says quietly, "Receive your sight." Three simple words, perhaps a touch, and Bartimaeus's universe floods with light.

There are two things we might consider. The first is Jesus' question. Once again the question is universal. Jesus is saying to us what he said to Bartimaeus, What do you want me to do for you? We all have innumerable needs, real or imagined. We might seriously consider placing those needs before Our Lord in some quiet moment. By the very act of doing so we will begin to separate imagined need from genuine need. The second focus for our thinking might come from a seemingly casual detail recalled by the gospel writer. He tells us that just before going forward to stand in front of Jesus, Bartimaeus threw off his cloak. It's intriguing to consider why he did that and why Luke recalls it years later. Whatever the reason may be, it is possible for us to take that quick, simple gesture, perhaps done in sheer exuberance that day on the Jericho road, and to make it a symbol of a significant need in our own lives.

The First Searchers

We owe almost everything we know about Jesus to the early communities of men and women who chose to follow him. Among those communities there were five people to whom we will never be able to repay our debt. About the lives of four of these people we know little, but what we do know is their deep commitment to Jesus as Lord, their obvious conviction that his life, death, and resurrection are of ultimate significance, and, perhaps most important of all, their intuition that what had begun in him was going to grow and deepen and affect human experience until the end of time. The names of these five people are Mark, Matthew, Luke, John, and Saul of Tarsus, later to be called Paul. Almost everything we know about Jesus we know through the minds and memories and writings of these five.

The very early community from which and for which Mark wrote felt that there was very little time ahead. They looked for Jesus to return as Lord of all within the lifetime of that first generation. In Paul's early years of ministry it sounds as if he felt the same. On the other hand Matthew and Luke, writing some years later, began to see the possibility that the Christian community, already growing across the empire, was going to need resources for a very long time as it served its Lord down the centuries. As we now know, they were right.

John, whose great gift was to intuit and to imagine and to dream, gives us two great insights. In his gospel he suggests that the return of Jesus takes place within the human heart. In his later book, which we call Revelation (and the last book of the New Testament), John uses a marvellous series of visions to help us see Jesus as the instrument of ultimate love and risen life through whom God forms and rules and gives meaning to all creation.

Mark, writing for the communities of Christians already formed, takes for granted that his readers regard Jesus as Lord. In that sense his book is not so much for Christian enquirers as for Christian believers. However, we have to remember that there are many Christians who have come to faith by reading Mark's book.

Matthew, however, has a different purpose. By the time he is writing the communities have spread. Leadership, teaching, and organization are going to be more and more necessary. Something is forming around the living, risen Jesus, something we call the church. As Matthew looks to the future he also has a rich sense of the importance of the past. He realizes that Jesus as a Jew was formed by the Jewish past, its forms of thought, its law, its traditions, its worship. That is why Matthew is always making links between moments in Jesus' life and past events in the Hebrew scriptures.

Luke is writing for an even larger world. By that time some Christians are realizing that Jesus Christ is too significant for anything smaller than the whole world. This outlook affects everything in Luke's two books; he wrote both a gospel and the book of Acts. For instance, where Matthew traces Jesus' family line back as far as Abraham, leaving it still within Judaism, Luke goes right back to Adam and Eve, telling us that he believes Jesus to be linked with the story of all humanity.

John was probably elderly when he wrote his books, and he too wrote for the whole world. As he prepares his book he searches for a way to begin so that he will get the attention of the great world of Greco-Roman civilization. John recalls how Greeks believe that there is a word at the heart of the universe waiting to be spoken, and he decides he will speak about Jesus in terms of that eternal Word. So he begins his gospel by announcing that the Word has been spoken. How? In Jesus' living out of human experience.

All of the men and women in those early communities, including the particular people we have mentioned, searched intensely for the meaning of what had happened in Bethlehem, Nazareth, and Jerusalem. Each gospel writer came to express the mystery and the meaning in his own way. Each was saying who Jesus was for him and for the whole community around him.

There is another author who did his own far-flung questing. It's easy to forget that though the four gospels are first in our Bibles, the first writings used widely by the early Christians were the letters that Paul began writing to the various communities he had brought into being and continued to care for. These letters or epistles vary. Some deal with particular problems developing in the community. One letter to a friend, Philemon, actually deals with a specific personal request about a runaway slave. On the other hand the great letter to the community in Rome wrestles with the whole mystery of human nature and our relationship with Jesus as Our Lord.

There are many other writers: we see their names in our scriptures. James wrote a letter. Someone we don't know wrote one to Hebrew Christians. Peter wrote to the Christian communities scattered across the empire. Even then the list is far from complete. There is of course a whole host of men and women who never wrote anything. Mary of Magdala disappears from the story as soon as we turn the last page of John's gospel, yet we can only imagine the intimacy and intensity of all she could have handed down. Then, the centurion at Capernaum, the young man cured of blindness, the woman Jesus met on the Lebanese coast whose child he cured. That spotlights only a few. Surely for all of them life went on. Surely for many of them the voice and face of Jesus remained fresh and vivid for the rest of their lives. Surely they often asked, just as we do, "Who is Jesus for me?" We can only assume that for them there were times when his Holy Spirit spoke to the depths within them. They began the quest; we are still on it; it will never end.

Encounters and Conversations

Because each one of us is an individual, nothing is more fascinating to us than other individuals. All our lives we are involved with other people, joyfully or painfully, lovingly or hatefully, personally or professionally. The good news that we call the gospel is that God, knowing our fascination with human beingness, decided that the only way to reach us was by God's becoming a person among us.

Because God became a person in Jesus, the gospel narrative is full of encounters between Jesus and other men and women. It is in these encounters that we discover the good news, because in a very wonderful way, we discover that they have become our own encounters with a Jesus who, suddenly and miraculously, is as much present with us as he was with the man or woman of whom we read.

To realize this power within the gospel narratives makes us approach them more and more expectantly. Our expectation will be that we are not about to contact a past reality but a present one. We are not about to meet a remembered Jesus, but a Jesus who is our contemporary.

The Prominent Politician

Suppose you are a brilliant scholar, a prominent politician. Suppose you have a good career carefully built up over a number of years. Suppose that you have carved out your place in society, that you are secure in your lifestyle and in your view of the world. Then suppose you meet somebody who challenges every aspect of who you are, what you have done, and all you hope for.

Who knows why Nicodemus and Jesus first met? Obviously it was at Nicodemus's wish and initiative. John tells us that he came to Jesus by night. We need to be quite clear about this man if we are to realize the power of the magnet that Jesus was for him. As a member of the Sanhedrin, the governing body of the Temple and, in effect, the whole country, Nicodemus had no need to go to anybody. He was already in possession of all the answers. Members of the Sanhedrin were not in the habit of asking country rabbis from Galilee for some time as a favour after office hours! In the world of Nicodemus, country rabbis, especially from Galilee, were at best a tiresome but necessary nuisance. There could be only one reason for this night-time meeting: Nicodemus had deep needs.

When they meet Jesus immediately intuits the void in Nicodemus. Jesus knows that whatever this man has come for it is certainly not more religious information or theological discussion. Nicodemus can get that anywhere at any time; so can we all, for that matter. But deep inside most of us there are places, empty places, where information and discussion give no satisfaction, no nourishment.

Jesus says quietly to Nicodemus that he must be born again. The phrase rocks his orderly world because it suggests that he has to go down into the depths of his being and touch again the eternal child within himself. Jesus has said many times to anyone who will listen that if we want even to glimpse the kingdom of heaven we have to rediscover the child within ourselves and look at reality through this child's eyes, recapturing what has been lost, things such as trust, love, innocence, a sense of boundless possibility.

In one quiet sentence the rabbi stands Nicodemus's neat ordered universe on its head. Seeing his bafflement Jesus decides to use another image. This time Jesus speaks of a wind, a wind that is as near as one's own breath, as warm as the winds of the desert, as mysterious as the spirit of God, a wind one can neither command nor control.

Actually we never know whether or not Nicodemus understands. But what do we mean by "understand"? How much do any of us really understand the terrible and beautiful mysteries of Christian faith? Times without number, when we act on some principle of Christian faith, we do so without understanding. It is as if something moves us, guides us, takes us, and we follow. What may move us is often elusive, undefinable. The echo of a parable told us when we were young, the remembered example of an elder, a story recalled, the memory of a hymn verse sung in some distant corner of time, these are the things that move us and call us to decide and to act in faith. As Nicodemus leaves there is not the slightest suggestion in the gospel that he understands. But it will become obvious that a seed has been sown in this man's deepest being.

The Sanhedrin is in session. The case in question is that of the rabbi who by now is showing signs of being a public nuisance, even a possible danger to the peace. Nicodemus stays silent as long as possible. He then risks questioning the process. Suddenly he is the dove among hawks. There is a silence. Then a learned colleague, careful as always to observe the rules of the house, lashes Nicodemus with the ultimate sneering reference in that society. "Are you from Galilee too?" he asks, meaning, "Is it possible that even you are politically unreliable?" Nicodemus is not reported as making any reply.

Sometime later, it is the dawn after a terrible day for Nicodemus. He has learned the hard way that it is possible to be in a position of power and to be politically helpless. He has watched as something ghastly was done in his name as a member of the political administration. He is appalled, shamed, without illusion, and without hope. He has kept his position at a high price. But then what would have been achieved if he had trumpeted his allegiance in the face of an establishment adamant about imposing its will? Nicodemus faces the great and complex moral question which each one of us faces at some time or other. In some sense we could say that we work it out daily: for all but the greatest of souls the bottom line is survival.

At this moment Nicodemus has a visitor — Joseph, a wealthy friend from Arimathaea. We don't know if either knew the other had any links to the dead Galilean. Nicodemus is asked if he will assist in the disposal of the body for which Joseph has offered a resting place. If he accepts, the news will be on an official desk within the hour. The action will not itself destroy him, but it will mark him as politically unstable, a euphemism for political death. His mind, honed for years to assess the subtleties of political survival, gauges the options. In that moment he glimpses again the child he was once fleetingly shown. He feels the breath of a warm desert wind bringing evening to Jerusalem. It sighs within him, carrying a voice, a presence, a memory. Suddenly Nicodemus knows that some things are more important than political survival. Together he and Joseph leave the office.

All over the world there are Nicodemuses. They assist in great decisions; they are present at moments of great social significance; they take part in events that often lead to headlines. What takes place at such times is not always the expression of the will of Christ. Our Nicodemuses know that. But their faithfulness may have succeeded in placing within events and changes and policies some seed of their Lord's love and hope and grace. Such ministries, often carried out in great ambiguity and under great pressure, are known to the Christ who is the Lord of history.

Encounter at Noon

The well is still there. Nowadays you go through a small gate, then walk along a narrow path near the roofless church until you come to the top of the steps. Then you go down into the cool darkness and the small grotto-like room festooned with religious bric-à-brac. If you wish to check the depth of the old well you purchase a small glass of water from the priest. Pouring it into the darkness you wait as the water drops down through the centuries.

Jesus waited by the well while the others went to get something for lunch. He was tired and probably he appreciated the solitude. Then the woman came out of the shimmering haze. Thank God she did, because you and I receive the gift of the wonderful encounter that occurred. Thanks to John's memory it now belongs to us forever.

The fact that she came at all said a great deal; at least to anyone aware of cultural nuances it hinted a great deal. It was high noon and she came alone to the well for water. That was far from normal, and Jesus immediately knows something is wrong. He asks her for a drink.

The woman is startled and wary. In these first few seconds two strong taboos are broken! Jews don't speak to Samaritans, and in circumstances like this men do not speak to women. In spite of her wariness something deep in her responds. Here is a man who is quite prepared to drive straight through taboos and conventions. She has had to deal with some taboos herself one way and another.

From the beginning she senses that there is in this man something more than she is hearing. He is not merely asking for a drink; he suggests that he possesses another source of refreshment, another kind of "drink." We need to listen with her kind of sensitivity as we ourselves encounter Our Lord. He is never offering us just religion, just theology, just church membership. He offers whatever we are thirsty for, inner peace, joy, challenge, vocation, meaning.

Jesus and the woman fence as two people do who are taking each other's measure, each enjoying the encounter. Jesus is quietly and gently persistent; the woman is intrigued but wary. This stranger is suggesting he can give her something, a quality, a resource for living. She is also aware that conversational intimacy leads to self-revelation and she has things to hide.

So have we all. We are wary of spiritual encounters, spiritual discussion, because all paths in search of the holy involve some measure of confession, some self-revelation.

Jesus knows how valuable it can be when a spiritual moment can be shared with someone, so he suggests she reach for someone to share what he has to offer: he suggests she bring her husband. For a long moment there is silence and obvious embarrassment. She says simply, "I have no husband." Sooner or later all encounters with Our Lord involve some measure of self-revelation even if only to ourselves. For a moment we see the hidden places, the unacknowledged agenda, the yawning gaps in the fabric of our lives.

Jesus pauses at her confession. He suggests the truth and she does not deny it: there have been a number of relationships. Interestingly she is neither angry nor distraught; sometimes acknowledging reality can be a relief. We can even feel grateful to the one who has risked hurting us to get us to this point.

Then the woman does a very human thing: she makes a valiant effort to change the subject. Ironically she chooses religion as less threatening than spirituality! She asks Jesus to give his opinion about a generations-long issue dividing Jew and Samaritan. Gently but firmly Jesus refuses to be drawn: he dismisses the issue as irrelevant. The woman makes one more effort to escape the encounter: she suggests that it will be pleasant to think about these things when the Messiah comes. In other words she uses the well-worn device we all use to avoid things of the spirit. Why not talk about all this another day, sometime when we are not so busy — any time as long as it is not now, because we are frightened at the possibility that we may encounter a powerful and compelling reality.

Again Jesus doesn't allow her an escape. He says to her what he says to all of us who encounter him at all our countless busy noon-hour wells. He says, "I who speak to you am he." Each of us decides what our response to that is to be.

The Outsider

The encounter between Jesus and Zacchaeus is such that it is not impossible it gave Dickens, consciously or unconsciously, the seed for *A Christmas Carol*. Zacchaeus has worked a Roman tax concession for years at the expense of his fellow townspeople, and has prospered. However, there has been a price to pay. He now receives the cordial hatred of all those around him. Some people are willing to pay that kind of price for money. Being hated and ostracized and rich can give a warped sense of power. The equation is simple if at times costly.

What was it about a single sharing of dinner that changed the equation for Zacchaeus? Maybe we should merely accept the fact that the guest that night was unique and leave it at that. But the interesting thing is that there is no effort in the gospel to make that evening into an example of explicit evangelism. All we have is the dinner dishes pushed aside and Zacchaeus blurting out his determination to reform. This is followed by Jesus' enthusiastic response: ''Salvation has come to this house.''

One would give a great deal to have been a fly on the wall that evening. The heavy heat of the Jericho day has turned to the cool of evening. Zacchaeus has presumably alerted his household about the distinguished guest — a guest who had offered to come. Guests in this house would tend to be only the small circle who, like Zacchaeus, depended on the Roman occupation for their income. Social life in such a small and beleaguered circle usually tends to be forced, based as it is on mutual survival. The whole group would be regarded as outsiders by the general population. The Romans rented out the task of getting in local tax money, and the highest bid from a local man got the franchise. He then set about gathering the taxes, making sure that he himself made a substantial cut on the side. Zacchaeus himself says he was good at his job and has done very well.

In Luke's subtle telling of this story there is something rather pathetic about Zacchaeus. The second and third verses are beautifully juxtaposed. Zacchaeus is both "chief tax collector and rich" but, alas, "small of stature." Add the final indignity of what is probably the real reason he could not see Jesus passing — the crowd by closing ranks in front of him and sniggering at his frantic efforts to get through — and we have a pretty pathetic picture.

The fact that Zacchaeus had put himself in this ridiculous situation at all is a measure of his determination to see Jesus. Here he is, an affluent if despised burgher of the town, balanced rather precariously on a tree branch, feeling rather idiotic and vulnerable if the truth were known, watching someone who is at the moment the object of public adulation. Suddenly to the astonishment of nearby listeners, and probably to their great resentment, the visitor reaches out to Zacchaeus and suggests dining together, an act not only of social intimacy but also sacred.

As we know, this act is typical of Jesus: the outsider is noticed and reached for. C.S. Lewis in his essay entitled "The Inner Ring" (*Transpositions and Other Addresses*, 1949) writes of the deep longing in everybody to be included, the dread we have of being outside what we perceive to be a circle of friendship, recognition, and influence. By this stage Zacchaeus must have developed some of the sad devices of those who in some way and for some reason have chosen to isolate themselves. There would be the pathetic pretensions of self-sufficiency, the claim to be able to live without friends, to be superior to the need for intimacy. Now we see a transitory intimacy offered by Jesus, and like the walls of Jericho in the old story, the sad self-defences of Zacchaeus crumble. As with Paul on the road to Damascus Zacchaeus was waiting for the removal of his mask.

Sometimes it is astonishing how easily the direction of a person's life can be changed if the right gesture or the right word is made at precisely the right moment! Very often the change has taken place long ago and is only waiting for someone to bring it to the surface. Sometimes it will need only a word, a crossing of paths, a time given to listen. We will never know how the conversation went that evening. It is very unlikely that it involved a great deal of sermonizing to Zacchaeus on Jesus' part. There is no evidence that Our Lord ever indulged in that. Luke tells us of only two short statements Jesus makes. Sometimes when we really do listen it turns out that almost nothing need be said. The person speaking has done it all. The listener has only to name joyfully what has been done. "Salvation has come to this house."

A Courageous Woman

Nowadays one passes Magdala in a moment or two. The road swings slightly inland from the lakeshore. There are some small buildings between the highway and the lake, and there is a glimpse of green rows in the plantation of the nearby kibbutz. Somewhere beyond the green, hidden from the sun by the growing things, are the last remains of the town buried in the brown, dusty earth. Here is the place where Mary lived and grew, and from here, one day, she left.

In that world the chances of a woman leaving her village or town were slim, except for marriage. However, there is no suggestion in the gospel that Mary was ever married; certainly, there is reasonable evidence that she was not married when she encountered Jesus of Nazareth.

There is no woman in the world on whom so much fantasy has been projected as Mary of Magdala. It has been said that history has given her a role she neither earned nor would have wanted. In effect her role has been to embody all aspects of womanhood not embodied by the Virgin Mary. For centuries the very name Mary of Magdala, often dramatized by changing it to "The Magdalene," has conjured up images of the exotic, the passionate, even the bawdy. The reformed prostitute is a theme beloved in Christian tradition. On the wall of the Orthodox Church of St. Gabriel in modern Nazareth there is a painting of Mary of Alexandria. She is shown as old and emaciated, accepting the sacrament from a bishop. As the story goes Mary was a prostitute who took ship to the Holy Land to ply her trade among pilgrims. While there she embraced Christianity and chose the life of a hermit in the desert. Thirty years later she was found, near death, and was asked what she wanted above all else. She asked for the sacrament. She and Mary of Magdala are archetypes in the complex sexual agenda of Christian imagination.

We know that Jesus healed Mary of Magdala of what the gospel story says were seven devils. Seven devils could mean merely many troubles or many elements of illness. We cannot be more precise than that. Really all we can say is that she met Jesus and the encounter changed her life. What we know subsequently of her role in the extraordinary days of Jesus' crucifixion and resurrection provides a portrait of a magnificent human being.

We know she was present at the execution; that in itself says a great deal. It took more than normal courage and stomach to watch a Roman execution. When we add to this horror the possibility that she loved the man being murdered before her eyes, we cannot imagine what fortitude it took to be there at all. Hours later when Joseph and Nicodemus took the body down, wrapped it, and stumbled away to the nearby tomb, she was still there watching. The next morning as dawn broke — the gospel says "while it was yet dark" — Mary was one of those who moved through the city gate to tend the body, an act of great courage for a woman in that society.

John the evangelist makes it perfectly clear that it was Mary of Magdala who announced to the rest of the community, and therefore to all the world and to the rest of time, that the tomb was empty. It was John who learned, presumably from Mary, of that moment in the dawn when she turned, saw a figure, thought it might be the gardener, and pleaded for information. She then heard her name spoken by a voice she had never expected to hear again. It is John who does not hesitate to tell us of Mary's instinct to embrace Jesus. I suspect she herself felt no reason to apologize for that.

Weeks later the community has gathered in Jerusalem. Over the intervening weeks Jesus' recurring presence among them has guided them there, and on a particular day to the Mount of Olives. Once again his visible presence is focused for them, but this time there is a mysterious sense of finality. This mysterious moment Christians call the ascension of Our Lord. Following the passing of his presence they return to Jerusalem. As they return Luke lets us see their faces going by us as he names them. When he has given us the list of those who were there he adds — ''All these with one accord devoted themselves to prayer, together with the women, and Mary the mother of Jesus.'' Although the name of Mary of Magdala is not mentioned, she was undoubtedly there, her face radiant.

The Homemaker

There is a remarkable lack of stained glass to her glory, yet if we were to ask Our Lord to furnish us with a list of those to whom he would like some stained glass to be dedicated, I suspect that he would place the name of Martha of Bethany high on his list. Think of those who did simple, warm-hearted things for us at some stage. Think of the person who invited us to a house and a dining-room table when we were away from home and rather tired of hotel rooms or, in earlier years, of school food. Think of someone who was always practical, sometimes a little blunt, but with whom you always knew where you stood, someone about whom you were not always having to wonder what mood they were in because they always seemed to be too busy to get into any moods, at least any complicated ones!

Rather typically, Martha walked into Jesus' life without asking. Luke has saved the moment: Jesus is "on his way" with some of his followers and they enter a village. There is a suggestion of homelessness. By this time Jesus is well known, and people tend to hang back from engaging someone who has become a public figure. The well-known media face, the prominent politician, are seen most often at a distance. Very often it will be someone of surprising modesty and ordinariness who approaches them. They come forward knowing instinctively that underneath the veneer of reputation and public image there is another human being, like themselves the product of home, school, family life. Martha, as Luke says, received Jesus into her house. There is no demure admiration from a distance, no precious presuming that this man is so spiritual that he might not need a good dinner and a roof for the night.

We meet this outgoing quality in Martha again. It is months later and her life has been shattered by her brother Lazarus's death. She has waited for Jesus to come. By this time he has become their friend, and instinctively she wants him with her in this agony. Jesus delays coming and when he does, John tells us, Martha "went to meet him while Mary stayed in the house." All her life Martha goes out to meet people. Perhaps that first day she instinctively saw in Jesus a person who was himself always going out to meet people and who therefore badly needed someone to reverse roles and to go out to meet him. Perhaps that's why John feels moved to add that "Jesus loved Martha and her sister and Lazarus."

There is a restlessness in Martha, even a hint of distractedness. We don't know why. The three of them, sisters and brother, were unmarried in that most marrying of societies. Were there shadows in their memories from their parents? Why was Martha always trying to set the world aright, to get it perfectly neat and ordered? Perhaps Martha, like many of us, had her demons, thus making it so good to discover this quiet stranger whose very presence was gracegiving.

She obviously felt totally at home with Jesus. There is no pretence, no hiding of real feelings when he appears after Lazarus has died. Like many of us in our grief Martha needs a focus for her anger. It may be an indication of her deep affection for Jesus that she makes him the focus. "If you had been here my brother would not have died," she says, bluntly and simply. We then hear her voice change as she voices a forlorn, impossible hope: "Even now I know that whatever you ask from God, God will give you." We hear her mood switching from moment to moment.

There is a hint of impatience at Jesus' initial efforts at reassurance. He says, "Your brother will rise again." Martha retorts, "I know that he will rise again in the resurrection at the last day." Is this a dismissal of well-meant theology? Then, equally quickly the dismissal dies away and we hear a different Martha. Now this magnificent woman affirms Jesus in a way that fully echoes the words of Peter at Caesarea Phillipi: "Lord," Martha blurts out, "I believe that you are the Christ."

Then the moment is cut off. The Marthas of this world rarely feel comfortable with intensity or self-revelation. For Martha that sort of thing belongs best to Mary. She turns away and brings her sister to Jesus. How unselfish is the way she does it. ''The teacher is here and is calling for you,'' she tells her sister, self-effacement in every word.

Time has passed. Lazarus lives and life goes on. Shadows are gathering about Jesus, and he comes again to Bethany. Again John captures the moment. ''Six days before Passover Jesus came to Bethany. There they made him a supper and Martha served.'' Of course it was Martha who served. That's what Martha always does; she is incapable of doing otherwise. That is why she walks from the pages of scripture into our lives, if we but open our eyes to see her beauty.

The Governor's Wife

Procula, the wife of the Procurator Gaius Pontius Pilate, appears only for a fleeting moment in the gospel. Strictly speaking she does not appear at all. She merely sends a message which emerges on to the stage of the gospel only because it is addressed to her husband while his court is in session.

The trial of Jesus is in progress. Actually, this is one of a series of quick trials, a series in which we have every indication that Pilate did his best to avoid getting deeply involved in what was to him an utterly and typically labyrinthine Jewish issue. Roman law, like the Roman mind, was best suited to straightforward practical issues of crime and punishment. What it detested was being forced to arbitrate in arcane and undefinable religious issues among occupied people. Where it was at all possible to do so Rome left such issues in the hands of local authorities, who of course remained finally answerable to the Roman administration on the spot. Above all, Rome insisted that the death penalty be kept solely as a Roman decision.

Procula, a Roman matron of considerable social prominence, knows this. She has grown up in one of the most politically involved families in Rome. It is an indication of Procula's political muscle that she is here in Palestine at all. Up to this present appointment of her husband, it has been forbidden for the wife of the procurator of Palestine to accompany her husband on his tour of duty. The posting was considered too dangerous. Procula had successfully challenged that rule. This fact alone says something about the quality of this woman.

Precisely because of her political awareness Procula must have had an agonizing sense of helplessness as she watched her husband being drawn deeper and deeper into the morass of this essentially Jewish issue. We know a great deal of what contributed to her sense of helplessness. She knew that her husband was deeply in debt to the vast monetary system run by the high priests. She also must have known that the remainder of her husband's career, up to this point a rather uneven one, depended on his handling Judea successfully. There was one criterion for success, keeping the peace by any means. Pilate's indebtedness and his professional vulnerability placed both of them into the hands of the very forces they were supposed to be governing.

Procula knows with the certainty of political experience and deep intuition that this trial is exactly the kind of thing she and her husband have always dreaded. This is an issue where Pilate can keep either his integrity as a human being and as a Roman aristocrat or his professional career, but not both. Procula has now to watch her husband being destroyed by the ambiguity that lies waiting for all who work in political systems and exercise power.

A measure of this courageous woman's agony is suggested in a deceptively casual phrase in Matthew's book. Matthew tells us that "while he [Pilate] was sitting on the judgement seat, his wife sent word to him." Roman military and diplomatic wives simply did not do that unless some desperation had driven them to break the very strongest conventions of their class.

It appears that Procula has had a nightmare about the trial in progress. The language of her message to her husband is fraught with intense fear and urgency: "Have nothing to do with that righteous man, for I have suffered much over him today in a dream." Typical of her character, she trusted enough in her intuition to share it even at the risk of offending the official rules and incurring the discipline of a spouse already under extreme tension.

Why did Procula take such extreme action? Among the many traditions of Christian piety there is one that suggests that she had come in contact with Jesus or someone in the movement. We will never know whether or not this conjecture is true. She may have had some contact with the prisoner, if only to eavesdrop in the hall where Pilate had his judicial sessions. Some contact, however slight, was needed to be the source of her dream. Whatever be the truth, Procula was right in her intuition: their lives never recovered after the trial. Pilate himself behaved so foolishly and so provocatively that one can detect a wish to self-destruction. Only a few years later Procula and he stood on the afterdeck of an imperial galley as it sailed out of Caesarea, taking them to Rome to face charges of maladministration.

Procula touches the gospel story for a fleeting moment. She did not succeed in changing the course of the Christian drama. It is intriguing but pointless to wonder what would have happened if she had. If she had lived to be an elderly Roman matron she would surely have become aware of a growing community in the city focused around the life and teaching of the prisoner whose cause she had once pleaded. On that fateful Friday she did not hesitate to express her conviction that he was ''a righteous man.'' It is intriguing to wonder whether Procula encountered Jesus once again, not in a dream but in a familiar circle of faces and voices sharing bread and wine in his name.

A Costly Commitment

To be a member of the Sanhedrin in the time of Jesus was to be a person of great power and influence. In every sense one had arrived, personally, socially, politically. There was nothing higher to be achieved. You might have an ambition to be High Priest. However, all the ability in the world counted for little in those stakes. You either belonged to one or two families of ultimate significance or you were prepared for a very dangerous game of collision with the reigning monarch and the Roman authorities. Apart from all this, membership in the Sanhedrin was all that a man could desire, certainly for those who did not themselves have it.

We mention "those who do not have it" because major political responsibility in any society and in any age, while it brings many pleasant perks, also brings with it an often brutal struggle for personal survival. In the Jewish Sanhedrin survival was no easy business. The fact that it was a religious body did not in the least lessen its being a political snakepit. The society itself was extremely volatile; it was split into endless factions. All positions on everything were taken with rigorous and unrelenting seriousness. Very rarely was there loyalty across the factions. Each of the parties in the system demanded conformity. To refuse to conform courted political destruction.

All this needs to be said if we are to begin to appreciate the kind of man we meet in Joseph, the Sanhedrin member who presumably commuted, as we would say today, to his office from the nearby village of Arimathaea. Even this fact, that Joseph lived outside the city, may indicate that for many reasons he preferred to distance some aspects of his life from his professional existence. Could it have meant even more? Could it have meant that in recent years he had felt a need to distance himself from a system which no longer had his wholehearted respect? This is possible but of course we can't be sure.

What is particularly intriguing is that, even though none of the evangelists say more than a sentence or two about this man, together their comments add up to a surprisingly full image. All four writers say that he was a member of the council. Matthew, with an eye for a balance sheet, says that Joseph was rich. It is also Matthew who mentions Joseph's allegiance most categorically. He says quite plainly that Joseph was "a disciple of Christ." Mark and Luke both express this more obliquely. While John says that Joseph was a disciple but "secretly," Mark says merely that Joseph was "looking for the kingdom of God." Luke repeats this and adds that Joseph was "a good and righteous man." Luke then adds an important fact not mentioned anywhere else. He says that "Joseph had not consented to their purpose and deed." That could mean either that Joseph had fought the decision of the council actively, not hiding his allegiance, or it could mean that he abstained.

All four writers tell us that Joseph went personally to Pilate and asked permission to take down the body of Jesus from the cross and have it prepared for burial. We have to try to understand the loathing with which a crucified criminal was regarded in that culture to realize the commitment and courage behind this action. Mark hints at the risk in the action when he says that Joseph "took courage and went to Pilate." By doing so he stepped into the white light of public view: he was now a marked man.

Yet Joseph did it, and by doing so he flushed out another of his colleagues on the council, none other than Nicodemus. It is John who tells us of Nicodemus's appearing at the scene to assist Joseph. Obviously Nicodemus has also thrown caution to the wind. For both of them this visit to this ghastly mound could be the end of every political ambition either of them had ever had. Yet here they are going about this last service to the dead Jesus. The corpse must literally be lifted off the spikes. Someone must take its weight as it falls forward. Someone must lower the pitiful object to the ground. As we read the scriptures and hear these realities described, often in no more than a single sentence, it is easy to forget that the commitment of such men as Joseph of Arimathaea and his colleague Nicodemus, as well as involving great personal risk, also did not allow for any physical squeamishness.

There is a touch of infinite tenderness in a detail that Mark gives us. He says that Joseph "bought a linen shroud and taking him down, wrapped him in the linen shroud, and laid him in a tomb." We have already seen how Mark, echoed later by Luke, says tantalizingly of Joseph that he "was also himself looking for the kingdom of God." One cannot help wondering at what moments in later years Joseph may have glimpsed that kingdom. As with so much else we cannot know. Meanwhile we might ask for grace that we may be as faithful and as courageous a servant of the living Christ as Joseph was to the dead.

Apostle and Friend

The people we have just met are bit players in the gospel drama. To say this is not to diminish their part in any way. Each one has become immortalized by the encounter with Jesus.

What we do not have is a full portrait of the person. We see someone behave in a certain way in one setting. We form an impression of them, and they pass out of our lives. There is no time to know them beyond that moment.

Of the few we get to know as personalities, the one revealed to us most clearly and endearingly is the Galilean fisherman, who was the very first companion Jesus ever reached out to. His name was Peter. We meet him in the gospel, we follow him through the book of Acts into the early years of the community, and we listen to him as he writes in his middle age to the very widespread Christian communities. Peter is utterly real, utterly human. That is why we are so grateful to him: he gives us all permission to be human too!

The Disciple

Of all the men and women who live in the pages of the New Testament, Peter, the disciple of Jesus, comes to us in vivid and sometimes heart-rending humanity. Peter is our brother in the gospel. He is the person into whose presence we could come with least embarrassment and least awe. He is as transparent as we are, as vulnerable, as impetuous, and, as with us, he regrets much.

We are told that one of Jesus' followers was a Zealot; his name too was Simon. But certainly there is much of the zealot in the temperament of Peter, also named Simon. Peter was really a nickname given him by Jesus when they first met. One has the feeling that of the two brothers to whom Jesus said, "Follow me," that day on the shore, it was surely Peter who first slammed down the nets and said his resounding Yes. At Caesarea Philippi, when Jesus asks the penetrating question, "Who do you say that I am?", that same question that every Christian must at some stage respond to, it is Peter who breaks the hesitant silence with, "You are the Christ!" On two occasions that we know of, once in the wind and spray of a lake storm, and once in the calm of the morning on the shore, Peter's first response to the presence of Jesus is to leap into the water and head out for his friend. In the first awful moments of Jesus' arrest it is Peter who explodes into action, grabbing a sword and lashing at a minor official in the group.

But as with us all, Peter's temperament has its weaker, shadier side. It is Peter who vehemently denies the approaching cost of what Jesus is saying and doing. One cannot help but suspect that the vehemence with which Jesus dismisses Peter's well-intentioned assurances — "This will not happen to you" — arises from the very depths of their friendship. It is as if Jesus feels most vulnerable to this affectionate and well-intentioned man, as if Jesus fears that he himself will succumb to the temptation unwittingly being offered by Peter to back away from the coming crisis. After all, it is to a dear friend that we look for advice. It is to a friend we listen most carefully when we have to make key choices.

It is Peter who is completely uncomprehending when Jesus comes across to him with water and towel to wash his feet. All his life Peter is the kind of person who directs, leads, gets things done, rallies others, uses his strengths. The idea that authority is rooted in servanthood is not something that Peter has thought of in his life. The paradox is that in the future those very gifts of strength, self-confidence, initiative, will all be his again, this time transformed by his relationship with Jesus. Peter will learn, as most of us need to and all of us find difficult, that serving does not involve weakness. The whole of humanity, replete with powers and gifts and achievements, is learning the harsh lesson that we must serve creation or die.

Before we can see Peter's strengths given back to him, we must first see them taken from him. As with us all, Peter discovers that in a mysterious way our strengths and our weaknesses are somehow linked to one another. It is Peter's strength which enables him to risk going to the High Priest's house when Jesus is taken there. It is his weakness, at least his self-perceived weakness, that makes him deny that he even knows the prisoner. There is an irony in Peter's denial of Jesus. The denial was necessary if he were to survive, but in Peter's own mind it was still a denial. It shattered him as a man, and, but for one thing, would probably have destroyed his capacity to lead the future community. That one thing may have been nothing more than the saying of two words, one of them his name.

In Mark's gospel three women go to the tomb to attend to the body of Jesus. They are given the stupendous news, and they are then told to ''tell his disciples and Peter that he is going before you into Galilee.'' Why the addition of the two words ''and Peter''? Would he not be the first to come? Perhaps he would. But it is equally possible that the old Peter is gone and in his place is the shell of a man, emptied of self-confidence, contemptuous of himself, deeply ashamed of his actions and decisions of the last few, terrible days. This Peter, as the risen Lord knows, needs to be called again.

The same risen Lord knows something that is eternally true of human nature to which Peter in his shame and agony is blind. Our Lord knows that there are times when human beings simply cannot regain self-esteem on their own. It must be given back to them. Even this act can fail unless the giving back is done with great sensitivity. In the gospel we are given the great privilege of being present when this giving happens, and it is moving and beautiful to see. But first we look at the moment when Jesus and Peter had their short sharp clash at that last supper. It was to be the first of a series of things over which Peter would probably agonize in the next few days.

The Royal Slave

We respond to different things in different ways and with differing degrees of intensity. Ask someone who has been present at an event what it was that stood out for them. They tell you. You then ask someone else, and hear something completely different from what you were told before, although something else may be recalled with great clarity. Such is human nature.

It is also human nature to be surprised at our own reaction. We are moving through a situation where we are relating with others — it may be a conversation, a committee meeting — and someone does or says something to which to our own astonishment we respond angrily. We realize that we are under considerable pressure and it took this seemingly innocuous thing to trigger it. Was that what was going on in the upper room?

Christian memory and imagination has probed the flickering shadows of this room for twenty centuries. Every word spoken, every gesture made, has been subjected to inexpressibly detailed examination. The nuanced meaning of the words "This is my Body, This is my Blood" have severed whole societies and made armies march. Yet there is another moment, another action, which may have been more astonishing to those who were present. Much that took place would have been totally familiar to all of them since childhood. The food on the table, the bread, the wine, nothing would have served to raise an eyebrow or start a question. But something did happen that raised more than an eyebrow. It provoked passionate protest until that protest was swept aside by a stern rebuke. One cannot help but wonder if this is the moment which Peter would particularly recall above everything else that took place at that supper. All were involved, but it was Peter's reaction and its effect on Jesus which set the tone for the rest of them.

At a certain point in the evening Jesus got up and left the table. Their group was small and they must have watched him as he moved. They knew this was no ordinary evening; fear of the unknown was in the air. Jesus himself communicated tension and fear if only with the intensity of the things he was saying. His words hinted of crisis and finality.

He went to the door, stooped down, picked up the towel and the water container, turned and came back towards the table. He stopped where Peter was sitting. He knelt down, flipped back the wide sleeve of his robe, and gestured to Peter to give him his foot. Only then did Peter realize what was happening. He reacted the only way he knew. His body, his voice, his eyes, all expressed an explosion of anger, surprise, embarrassment, almost revulsion. "Lord, do you wash my feet? . . . You shall never wash my feet." Yet what startled the rest of them even more was Jesus' reply. It was not so much a reply as a quick, short, tongue lash. For a moment there was steel in his voice. To hear it in the room reminded them all of the moment in Caesarea Philippi when Peter had fervently wished away the threatening realities Jesus had just spoken of. Now, as then, all gentleness seemed to leave Jesus; every word rang with authority. "If I do not wash you, you have no part in me."

The words hung in the silence; each remained motionless. Then, slowly, Peter extended his foot. He spoke in a low, hushed voice, quite unlike his usual heartiness. "Lord, not my feet only but also my hands and my head." One by one they continued to extend their feet as he knelt before them. He took each foot gently, deliberately, as if he were receiving not part of them but all of each of them. None spoke. Jesus finished the task and replaced the vessel and the now grimy, dust-stained towel. He returned to the table, sat down, and began to speak to them.

Their thoughts went back to just a week or so before when they had spent the night near Jericho. Angry and hurt, Jesus had suddenly called them together. Speaking vehemently he pleaded with them to remember that true authority among them would always be based on servanthood and not on power. He was really offering them his own kind of authority. Only later did they learn about the selfish request of James and John for personal preferment. Now as he spoke to them in the context of this meal, they understood. This time he had acted out utter servanthood. What he had just done was the duty of the lowest slave in a household.

Perhaps it is in this servanthood that Jesus asks most from us. Very few of us find servanthood attractive, so few in fact that when people become servants for the sake of the gospel we are awed and often call them saints.

A Small Betrayal

It would have taken about twenty minutes for the group to walk from the upper room to the gardens on the lower slope of the Mount of Olives. After they had crossed the narrow valley of the Kidron just east of the city, Jesus suggested that the main group stay where they were; it was his pattern, particularly at times of pressure or tension. By now it was taken for granted in the band that Peter, James, and John were bound together with him in a special relationship, and, on the whole, the twelve understood and accepted it. It was even reassuring because it made him more human, like themselves. Typically, the recent disappointment with James and John had not changed his pattern. The four figures detached themselves from the group and moved further up the slope and deeper into the trees.

Among the four nothing seems to have been said as the darkness deepened around them. It seemed as if he and they were acting out a deep animal instinct, seeking the safety of the trees, lying as low as possible in the face of danger. They realized this even more when Jesus broke the silence. It was a single sentence, both an admission of how he was feeling and a command: ''My soul is very sorrowful even to death; remain here, and watch.'' They stood there for a moment, and then someone suggested they lie down.

They could see Jesus against a large rock in a tiny clearing, crouched down on his knees. He had not gone much farther. It seemed as if he had suddenly realized the futility of taking refuge. It was obvious he could no longer control the agony of fear; it was in his voice, a hoarse, infinitely weary pleading. Once it began it went on and on, pouring out of him. Afterwards, they were never sure how long they had been there. One of them who had stayed awake longer than the others said that there came a moment when the agony seemed to peak. Then, his voice changed, his body relaxed. It was as if he were handing over to someone. They had seen him do it before, after the crowds had gone, exhaustion etched on every line of his face. They would see him at a distance, alone with his Abba, reaching out and up, relaxing, drawing energy from a total intimacy which they recognized, and wondered at, and envied.

Suddenly, the three of them were aware of his presence among them. At first, confused and half awake, they could not make out what he was saying. When they realized the contempt in his voice they were devastated, it was so totally unlike him. It wasn't so much rage, it was bitter resignation. They never forgot the words, bitten out in the darkness: "Are you still sleeping and taking your rest?" Long after, they still writhed at the memory of that first betrayal.

Whether we realize it or not we have all slept in the Gethsemanes of other people. We have all failed them in times of their great need. The teenager moving through the emotional storms of those years, desperate for endless midnight outpourings, finds a parent already wearied by a long day. A distraught patient, nervous and worried by a midnight stab of pain, finds a doctor exhausted, dismissive, impatient. A man or a woman fighting alcohol or depression or any of the demons we can meet on our journey, comes to share all with a familiar priest only to find someone who is him or herself drained, unresponding, unhelpful. All such moments echo the bitter disappointment of Our Lord in Gethsemane.

We have all played both roles in our time. We may have been the one who failed to keep vigil, not because we did not want to but because we simply did not have anything more to give. We may have been the one who felt deserted and let down, and we may still carry the resentment. Whatever role we have played, our experience links us to Gethsemane: we taste the humanity and the limitations of those men nearest to Our Lord. In our guilt it may help to realize that Our Lord accepted the friendship and the service of those men in spite of their very obvious shortcomings. He loves us the same way, in our humanity. If on the other hand we have been the one neglected in our time of need, if we still feel that resentment, we also know that Our Lord understands what we feel. He felt our anger and disappointment and bitterness, and he expressed it. He also forgave, accepted, was reconciled, and asks us to do the same.

A Morning Encounter

The place of meeting between Peter and the friend he feels he has betrayed takes place on a section of the shoreline of the lake they both called home. It is dawn, and a thin column of smoke climbs against the background of hills not fully emerged from the morning mist.

We are about to witness the reintegration of a group of human beings. The community has been traumatized and immobilized by the terror and wonder of what they have experienced. Peter's voice is dead, and impassive, as he decides to go back fishing. As the others respond we can hear the same loss of purpose in their lives. Eventually, as with all of us after great shock and loss, they will have to get their lives back together again, but at this moment it requires a supreme effort to think about doing anything. They gather their equipment and set out in one boat. Why only one boat? In the face of sorrow or catastrophe it is very human to close ranks, to cluster.

Among them Peter is struggling with an almost incalculable weight of guilt, what he perceives as his own abject failure. That sense of failure is all the more terrible because of the expectations and self-image that Peter has always had. The leadership of this group has come naturally to him, and he has taken to it quite naturally. Moreover, Jesus' statements and actions have affirmed these self-perceptions. Peter has now come to realize, with brutal clarity, that he has never come to terms with the shadow side of those strengths. No moment has revealed this to Peter more clearly than the exchange with Jesus on the night when supper was shared and Jesus had spoken about the approaching doom.

Jesus had simply but chillingly warned them they would break under the strain. Peter could now recall his own response. It flooded back with an intensity that appalled him. Time after time in the trance-like days after the execution and the resurrection he had recalled his own blustering, his denying of even the possibility that he was as vulnerable as anybody else.

This time the dreaming was interrupted by a flurry of movement in the boat. Voices were raised, some coming up from sleepiness after the long night. Some pointed at the shore, still half hidden by the mist. Then John shouted in mingled disbelief and joy, "It is the Lord!" Peter tore at his clothes, flung himself over the side and headed in to shore.

Then he and Jesus had moved down the beach, distancing themselves from the others. He had experienced the most extraordinary hour with the risen Lord. Three times Jesus had asked him the same question, "Do you love me?" Three times Peter had responded. At first he had been taken aback, then mystified, finally puzzled and indignant, even hurt. Three times the direction had come from Jesus, "Feed my sheep." Then it finally dawned on Peter what was happening. He remembered something Jesus had said in the upper room, and his refusal to hear it. Now he heard Jesus clearly, and he felt an immense release.

In that upper room Jesus had tried to warn Peter he would experience deep failure. For Peter that failure had come suddenly in his efforts to escape detection in the courtyard of the house where Jesus was being questioned. Ever since, Peter had lived with the shame. Now, as he faced his living Lord on the shoreline, he recalled that Jesus had given him an order. He realized now that he had never heard the deep trust which the order implied. "Simon," Jesus had said, "Satan demanded to sift you like wheat, but I have prayed that your faith may not fail. When you have turned again, strengthen your brethren."

Now, on the shore, in telling him to "Feed my sheep" Jesus was giving him back his vocation to lead and to guide and to strengthen the others. The time had come when this work was needed. Jesus wanted none other than he, Peter, to do it. His failure was irrelevant to Jesus. What was significant was that Peter, chastened and matured by his own failure, was even more valuable material for the Lord's work.

This shoreline is a universal place. At some time or other we all stand here broken by a sense of failure. At such times our world is a place where we stumble and grope because we are aware that our pride has been humbled and our self-esteem shattered. We do not feel there is anything worthwhile ahead: we have failed.

But there comes towards us on this shore one who asks us to consider a choice. He points out to us that we can either continue to condemn ourselves, thus wasting the energy and gifts we still have to offer, or we can listen to Our Lord, who has already long forgiven our failure. If we do listen we will hear him setting us to the tasks he wishes us to perform for him, tasks which he knows we can do, for he himself gives us grace to do them.

The Leader

Peter is now middle-aged. He has become a very different person from the fisherman for whom the north end of the lake was the whole world. Ironically, it is still a ring of cities around a sea but this time it has grown vast and cosmopolitan. Peter's sea is now the Mediterranean, the sea he would have referred to in his childhood as the Great Sea, the sea around which the vast power of Rome rules. Once these cities were distant and mysterious; now many have become familiar to him. He has sailed into their bustling harbours, met with the groups who are always there to welcome him and to give him loving and respectful hospitality.

For these Christian men and women all across the empire Peter has become a rock of stability in a time that is becoming dangerous and unpredictable. Peter is their link with the small world of the lake, the keeper of the story that is sweeping across the world.

He has also discovered something he would not have thought possible before encountering his Lord. Recently he has found himself in the houses of the rich and powerful. He has learned that such people are human and have needs. Touched by the news of the gospel they too have begun to be drawn into Christian communities. Peter has come to understand the emptiness of some of their lives. He has come to know what makes them so pathetically eager to learn more of the way of Jesus.

As he thinks of men and women in high places Peter feels again his recent sense of foreboding that the small Christian communities might soon need people in high places. Suspicion is rising here and there in various regions of the empire.

It is not a concern about a new religion; Rome could not care
less for a person's private religion. What matters is whether
people might begin to long for some ultimate value or hope
or vision of society that might challenge the empire — always
the cause of official watchfulness.

Confidential reports are brought to faceless administrators
who duly forwarded them in sealed packages on the sleek
imperial galleys bound for Rome. Recently, Peter has received
reports of violent incidents. The heads of households have dis-
appeared, reappearing with marks on their bodies and fear in
their eyes. Some are beginning to withdraw from the circle
of the bread and the wine, and are returning to the laughter
and games of the official public holidays. These occasions sometimes involve the obligatory placing of the small offering in
front of the emperor's bust. That way, life is made easier, one's
wife and children are not harassed, one's job is safer, perhaps
even one's life. Faith in the god of the Christians could become
very costly.

Peter remembers how it all once seemed so simple, even
euphoric — the sense of growing camaraderie, the sense of
being special. In those early days, if any of them were questioned, they would just mumble some vague response and then
pass the responsibility on to Jesus. Now there was no such
escape. The increasingly anxious questions of the faithful have
to be responded to. Since those days he and the others have
had to search and argue and experiment to find out what Jesus'
words meant. More puzzling was all that had happened, the
supper where so much was said, the terrible ending on the hill,
the inexpressible reality of the living Lord. How in God's name
could any mind encompass these mysteries, any poor words
express them. Yet Peter knows he must try. People are demanding statements, explanations, plans. These things are not really
his gift; such things are Paul's gift, he thought. Peter feels
tired. Yet letters must go out to these enquirers. The thing
was to get the time.

We who are the children of Peter's faithfulness, looking back
from a future he could hardly imagine, know that he not only
tried to write something, he succeeded. He wrote to those scat-

tered communities and thereby gave them a great gift. He could not know then that some of the things he wrote would be words of grace to a culture far off in the twentieth century. That culture, like Peter's, would be feeling the pressure of a large surrounding society that cared little for Christian faith. In the late twentieth century the risk of physical abuse and torture would not be great for most Christians. There would, however, be societies where that reality was only too possible. There would be shootings and stranglings and torture which would try to silence Christian witness. All this Peter would have understood. It was happening in various parts of the empire in his lifetime. He himself would meet violence. But his words shone through to his contemporaries as they do to us.

"The end of all things is at hand. Keep sane and sober for your prayers. Hold unfailing your love for one another. . . . Practice hospitality ungrudgingly. . . . As each has received a gift, employ it for one another . . . whoever speaks . . . whoever renders service . . . [do it] in order that God may be glorified in Jesus Christ."

Peter's plea to us is to offer all that we have and are to the present age, seeing this time and society we are in as the arena of our service to God. We are not to waste time and energy wishing for a simpler past or a neat, ordered, safer future, but to see that the present is where our challenge lies. God's time is the present. Peter said his Yes in what was his present: God asks for our Yes now.

Remembering

We have tried to encounter the older Peter. Naturally, we cannot really know his thoughts and feelings. But in a troubled time we know that he must have felt the concerns that we would, that he must have often looked back as we do, because Peter, especially, is so human throughout the New Testament. Peter knew what Paul once called "the care of all the churches." He must have thought a great deal about the life of the Christian communities and the pressures they were under.

Anyone who has said a life-changing Yes knows very well that it is possible to spend the rest of one's life discovering and growing into what that Yes really means. Again Peter thought back to that very first day on the shore. The stranger had come along and they were surprised when he stopped. They might just as easily have given him short shrift. Yet he recalled how life seemed to begin in a completely new way at that moment. That conversation had been followed by others, conversations had gradually become companionship, companionship had gradually brought commitment. And what had the commitment eventually become? A cross.

Now, all these years later, that seemingly casual decision of his, his brother Andrew, and later their friends James and John, had grown into so much. Could all this pulsating, spreading life across the empire really have come from something so simple? Jesus had often referred to something as small as a grain of mustard seed that grew into a vast tree. What if he, Peter, and Andrew had said No? Would it have happened anyway? But through someone else's Yes?

What comes to pass because of the Yes or the No we all say in life, again and again? Yes to the love of this person rather than that person. No to this university and Yes to another.

Our choosing all seems so random, a jigsaw puzzle of acceptances and rejections, things done and not done, and yet when the jigsaw puzzle is assembled and life has been lived, there is for better or for worse a face on the other side of the assembled pieces, and quite literally only God knows what the total of Yes's and Nos has added up to within the total fabric of creation.

For Peter there is undeniable evidence of what has come from his first response. In all these cities, communities of faith in Jesus now exist. Sometimes the groups are small and fragile, some even fractious and at times unpleasant. Peter has learned in so many ways that while the Lord Jesus called his followers to perfection very few including himself approach even the outer ramparts of that delectable city! But what Peter has also learned, again and again, is that something else always comes into being among people because of the Lord's grace.

Peter realizes again that the secret of Jesus' call to a person is that it is not a call to an obsessive searching for perfection, with all the self-righteousness that this can bring. Rather it is a call to a loving community where the acceptance of the humanity of each member becomes possible. However, even in the early days Peter often saw that just because communities gather about the things of God, there is no guarantee that everything will always be sweetness and light. It made him smile to hear those early days romanticized among the new generation of Christians. As the world they were all facing became steadily more complex and more demanding, there was a tendency to look back with nostalgia to the world of the lakeside, its little towns, the flapping sails heading for the quayside, the cornfields golden on the hills. All of it, at least from this later vantage point, seemed so safe, so manageable, so innocent.

Peter remembered those early days when things were anything but innocent and safe. The terrible days of tension and fear leading to the final horror of the cross. The years of foundation laying that followed, of dealing with community problems and endless questions, of trying to respond to invitations and responsibilities of every conceivable kind, of summoning up the energy to keep going.

Thus it might have been with the aging Peter. He would always in a sense be the same Peter: all of us change yet remain the same. Peter the follower had become the leader, yet he would remain the follower of his Lord to the end of his days. When those days ended, and there is every indication they ended painfully and violently in martyrdom, Peter would still be able to say what he had once blurted out emotionally in far away Caesarea Philippi: "You are the Christ." Simple as that. He realized now how far from simple it was: it was the greatest mystery in the world. He knew only one thing about it: it was true.

Claims and Consequences

I hope you are now getting near to the beginning. If that seems a strange thing to say when we are obviously quite a way through this book, perhaps I should explain. While we are not far from the end of this particular book, there is a more important book about to begin — yours.

Malcolm Muggeridge was fond of saying that there are really three testaments, the Old Testament, the New Testament, and one's own testament. He was quite right. I often think that the proof of this lies in the peculiar way in which almost all the books of the New Testament end. The fact is that they all end with beginnings.

All four gospels end with the disciples realizing that — whatever it is — and they are not sure! — it is now up to them. The book of Acts ends with Paul still rushing around, preaching, writing, beginning new things and ideas. All the epistles end in effect — "over to you now." Then the book of Revelation looks forward into the future for the coming again of Jesus. Christian faith suggests that only when that happens will the real story of the universe begin, or at least the very best part. Your life and mine, lived in faith in Jesus, prepares for that future and helps bring it about.

Back to the Future

Our Christian faith began with events that took place nearly two thousand years ago. These events are our roots and we must never forget them. The ceaseless handing on of these roots is the work or the ministry of each generation of Christians.

However Christians can fall into the temptation of looking too much toward the past. The Bible tells the story of Lot and his wife fleeing from the destruction of their city. Lot's wife looks back and, as the ancient story puts it, becomes a pillar of salt. We presume that she is overtaken by either the fumes or the dust of the volcanic eruption. For century upon century that story has been heard as a warning to us all about the unfortunate consequences that can come from too much looking back!

If as Christians we want to encounter Jesus in his own time we simply cannot get back to Our Lord himself. The furthest we can get is to those men and women who walked and ate and travelled and argued with him. There are some who would say that we cannot get back quite that far. They would say that we can only get back as far as the four people who wrote about the first early community around Jesus.

It is through their eyes that we see Jesus, through their words that we hear him. They have relayed to us some of the countless things he said, the stories he told, the miracles he did, the healings, the encounters with people — all the memories that circulated in the early communities.

Today a Christian is in the position of a person who goes to a movie about a central character who never actually appears on screen. However, this figure will dominate the story because we constantly see the reaction of others to that presence. Our Christian experience is rather like that. If we want to experience the Christ of the gospels, we do so through the experience of those who respond to him and interact with him.

To do this it is quite right, even necessary, for us to go back in time, back to the gospels. We are not for a moment saying that a Christian should not explore the tradition; we must never cease exploring it. But as we go back to the lakeside and the hills and the towns which Jesus knew, we must realize that if we are going to encounter Jesus we must start looking into the faces of the men and women who in their own time encountered him. From their varied responses we learn more and more what it was like to encounter him. From looking at Thomas's agonized face I learn what it means to doubt Jesus. From looking at the face of Mary of Magdala I learn what it is like to love him. From looking at Peter I learn what it is like to be devoted to Jesus and yet continually to make mistakes in following him.

Having looked at these people in the gospel let's walk forward in time, forward into what is their future, although it is still our past. We are now walking from the gospels into the book of Acts. I watch Paul's face as he tries to deal with his lifelong guilt for persecuting the followers of Jesus. I watch him as he tries to give expression to the real meaning of Jesus' death and resurrection. I walk further into the passing decades until I see Peter again, now elderly, experienced, travelled, respected, trying to express for thousands of scattered communities what it means to follow the Jesus of the gospels. Walking on further towards the future, we see John on the island of Patmos. We watch his elderly eyes as they seek to express his vision of Jesus as the Lord of history.

Walking in this way from the past into the future is not for a moment leaving Jesus behind. He is with us in the experience written in the faces and lives we are encountering. Here is Anthony, in the Egyptian desert, silently contemplating. Here is Augustine saying Yes to following Jesus in the disintegrating world of the fifth century. Here is Julian saying her Yes to Jesus in the terrible fourteenth century. Here in our own century are Teresa in the filth of Calcutta, Bonhoeffer in his lonely cell, Romero in the brutality of San Salvador, Yanani Luwum in the awfulness of Idi Amin's Uganda. As we look at them, they are looking to Jesus. All of them are drawing on his grace and power to life sacrificially, to love passionately, and to hold on to faith triumphantly.

Perhaps we need to emphasise once again that in this image of returning to the gospels and then turning and walking back toward the future we are not in any way walking away from Jesus. We walk with him on the road back to the future. We meet many on that road. In them Jesus is utterly present, utterly contemporary.

Follow Me

There is so much to be learned from even the simplest and seemingly most casual statement of the gospel. Jesus called twelve disciples — a piece of information, nothing more. Yet it is very much more because it is like a stone dropped into a pool: the fact ripples in the mind. We see faces and hear voices. The names are familiar: Peter, James, John, Judas. Even though we have never seen them they seem familiar. I know Peter, so do you. We have both met him in our imaginations, although if we should compare our imaginings we might be amazed at the difference.

Jesus called disciples. Perhaps the most important thing to say after that statement is that he still does and he always will. Even if only from the fact that you and I meet on this page we can both assume that Jesus either has called or is calling both of us. How have we to this point responded to his call? Perhaps as we look at those whom Jesus called long ago, we can take comfort.

What may give us greatest comfort is the fact that they were all so very ordinary human beings. Not one of them come to us as hero or genius or in any way larger than life. We have only to be in their company in the gospel for a very short time to realize that Our Lord is not averse to the very ordinary.

Their origins are so ordinary. One cannot but help have the feeling that there must have been at least fifty other possibilities along the shoreline of the sea of Galilee on that day that Jesus said "Follow me" to Simon and Andrew. That possibility is salutary as we think about our being called. Maybe there are fifty others who might have been called instead of us. For all we know they may have prospered the cause of the Lord in today's world far more than we ever will. But Simon and Andrew and you and I are called and there's an end of it, or rather, there is the beginning of it for each of us.

Even their sins were ordinary. None of them sins romantically and magnificently. They are sinful in the run-of-the-mill, pedestrian ways that most of us are. There is a type of modern thriller where the villain will do evil on a cosmic scale. His or her lusts will be insatiable, their greed beyond measure, their reach will be planetary. Ironically this magnitude attracts us, perhaps because of its utter unreality. On the other hand real sinfulness is what we see in the disciples and in ourselves. Petty betrayal, bickering over position, fearful denial, jealousy in relationships. Sins like that are numbingly ordinary, and for that very reason we can identify with the sinners.

But Jesus went on calling such people to his side. Three years later when familiarity and intimacy had revealed every battered shred of their only too obvious humanity, he still called them and kept them near him and loved them. Even after they had scattered to the four points of the compass when he really needed them, Jesus never gave the slightest indication that he ever regretted that moment on the beach with James and John or that day in the tax office with Levi when he said, "Follow me." What that says to you and to me is that we can assume that Jesus does not regret calling us, whatever each of us has made or failed to make of our calling to this point.

Many of us have a wonderfully illogical way of dealing with our relationship with Jesus Christ, especially in later life. We may be in our middle or even later years, our capacity for faith tattered and fragile. Something may happen to remind us fleetingly of a long-ago relationship with Our Lord, a stage in our lives when he was very real and near to us, perhaps in childhood or adolescence or early adulthood. That nearness may have long faded for many reasons: busyness, disappointment, cynicism, intellectual rejection. The devil has the most wonderfully varied selection of subtle devices to undermine our relationship with Our Lord, and most of them pander to our pride, our ego, and our self-image.

But when a memory comes back, over the years, of a time when our relationship with Our Lord meant much to us, interestingly we often say something like — "Well, even if I did feel and think that way long ago I've made such a mess of things that there's nothing for it except to get on with my life." We don't realize that this device too is slipped into our mind by the old master of all such devices that kill the human spirit and separate us from faith.

The call of Our Lord is just as real now as it ever was or ever will be. Jesus has all sorts of possibilities for us to explore. He has innumerable good things for us to find in ourselves, in our relationships, in our professional lives, in the world of our time with all its problems and all its challenges. Jesus didn't just call disciples long ago. Jesus calls disciples now: I can be one, so can you. After all, I'm sure both of us are ordinary enough to apply!

The One Who Calls

The fact that Our Lord called the twelve disciples to be his apostles can sometimes make us forget that in other ways he called many other men and women to follow him. Too easily, we can embrace some overly neat exclusions, the commonest one being that because there is no woman among the apostles, therefore, women are not called to ordained ministry. One sometimes cannot help wondering if tradition has not placed on that small circle of men more precise definition and identity than it can bear.

On frequent occasions Jesus himself seemed to imply that in his mind there was a hierarchy of intimacy within the twelve. More than once it is Peter, James, and John who accompany Jesus on some significant occasion. One thinks particularly of the mysterious hours we have come to call his transfiguration. It is difficult to understand the reason for the exclusion of the main part of his band of followers from this experience. Anything we know today about the dynamics in any group suggests that such selection was not helpful to their subsequent relationships. Interestingly this inner group does not include Andrew, Peter's brother, and among the very first chosen. We never take these things as in any way a denial or a diminishment of the discipleship of some of them, although being human it is quite possible they may at times have felt slighted.

We tend to think of Jesus calling all his disciples in the way he called the first four. That call is sudden and unexpected: one moment they are working, the next they are following him. Ironically, this fits our western tendency to place our religion in one sanction of life and our work in another! But from anything we know about Christian vocation we realize that working and following Jesus are not necessarily different things. Our Lord can be and is followed by millions of men and women in the doing of their daily work. However, the traditional image of the call of the disciples may lead many gifted lay men and women to feeling that their call to follow Our Lord necessarily involves ordination.

We see another kind of calling in Jesus: it is not so much a call as an invitation, an acceptance of the response a person has already made to him. Suppose your name is Mary, that you live in Magdala on the west side of the lake, and your life has been put back together by this man from Nazareth. He has given you a new focus, a new sanity, a new wholeness. In turn he seems to welcome your companionship, so much so that when you have moved through the horror of that terrible Friday, when you go looking for his poor, butchered body, he will encounter you in a way given to none other. He will name you, and you through tears of mingled joy and grief will name him Master. Does the development of that intimacy and that bonding not constitute the most genuine calling to follow him? In fact we might do well to contrast this call with the formalized process which later gives Matthias an official apostleship so devoid of consequent significance that not a single word is attributed to him and not a single event told involving him!

Suppose your name is Simon and you are North African. You spend your savings on a trip to Jerusalem. One minute you are minding your own business in a crowded street and the next you are being dragged forward by a Roman military squad to carry the ghastly crosspiece for a collapsing prisoner totally unknown to you. Suppose, however, there is something about him that haunts you, and one day you come in contact with a group of people who drink wine and eat bread in his name. Suppose you tell your two young sons about him and that one day they become leaders of the movement. None of this is impossible and all of it is a part of long, Christian tradition. Has not Our Lord called you to discipleship in its fullest sense?

Suppose your name is Saul, implacable enemy of Jesus of Nazareth. One day at the height of your powers you are traumatized and blinded by a sense of his presence. You have such a sense of call that you refer to yourself as "the least of all the apostles," but nevertheless an apostle. How many countless men and women can attest to their being called with equal blinding clarity and certainty?

Each of us is the least of Jesus' apostles. Was there a beach and a stranger and the words "Follow me" when you were called? I doubt it, although there may well have been a stranger. There may have been no one moment for you; on the other hand, this very moment, on this page, is such a moment. Personally, I can recall faces and voices and incidents and friendships which I now realize were given to me as disguised encounters with Jesus, and so it is with all of us. He may come disguised as an acquaintance, as a professional colleague, as a stranger met casually at a conference. He may come as a book lent to us, or as the voice of one of our children. He can come in any unguarded moment and in spite of all our defences. He can come to us in the nourishment of bread or in the fire of wine. But he is always saying the same thing — Follow me. And all we have to say is Yes and life becomes something new. It becomes a gift to be received and at the same time given away.

The Presence of Jesus

Suppose we could speak with one of the men and women who shared the years of Jesus' public ministry, the terrible days of the last week in Jerusalem — the realization of his living beyond the horror of the cross, and eventually sharing the mysterious moment of the ascension.

Suppose, rather like a modern TV reporter, we could ask them about their succession of experiences. There is a sense in which we have already had this done for us because the gospel writers give us the distilled experiences and memories of the early communities. But let us try to express what one of those men or women might say, expressing it in our own way yet trying to remain true to the gospel.

They would probably begin by telling us of their first encounter with Jesus, where it was and how it happened; we all tend to dwell on beginnings and endings. They might then tell us of various experiences they had with him over those few years. We would certainly hear of some events which we already know from the gospel record; we would equally certainly be told things that never became part of the common memory. However, whatever we heard would be very much set in the everyday world of that time, the world of the lake, of boat prices, fish catches, sheep markets, of sick relatives and friends, of family and financial problems. Sometimes we would hear of moments when they felt a sense of mystery and even awe in the presence of Jesus, but even these moments would be set in the everyday. Always there would be the necessary things of human life, pain, laughter, tears, arguments, wonderings about what was going on, thoughts and doubts and fears and hopes about where it was all leading.

Then they would tell us of the gradually increasing conflict. First the harsh questions, then the arguments, then the insults, then the enemies, then the awful last days, and finally the nightmare on the hilltop. They would speak of the sense of utter loss and failure and ending. Then — as they speak to us, their voices change; they begin to grope for words. He was alive — that above all is what they would say. But then they would hesitate and grope again. He was alive and he was there among them and he was utterly and wonderfully real — and yet, there was a difference. He was the same, yet he had been changed. It wasn't that he was in any way less real than he had always been; if anything, he was even more real. He had moved beyond them but had returned to them. It seemed to be a different order of reality, so much so that there were times when they knew him and yet did not know him. Then something would happen, as if he accommodated himself to their limited sight, and then with immense joy mingled with a kind of awe, they would know him.

That kind of presence, they would tell us, continued for some time. They experienced it around Jerusalem, then, later, in Galilee. Long afterwards Paul made a list of those occasions when both groups and individuals became aware of Jesus' risen presence. Some very personal needs were dealt with, especially in the cases of Thomas and Peter and perhaps Mary of Magdala; at other times Jesus addressed them as a group. Then, this way of being among them came to an end.

They would then tell how it ended, how Jesus spoke of the future and then went from them. We must be content with their groping images. "A cloud hid him from their sight," reports Luke. Then they began to do what he told them to do: to wait, but for what they didn't really know.

The day the waiting ended he came to them in a totally new way. They didn't see him; instead, they saw him in each other. They felt him as fire in their hearts, a bonding they had never felt before. They felt him speaking through them with an effect beyond their comprehension. On that day the early Christian community, which only some weeks before had been directionless and without hope, became energized and directed out beyond itself. That day, eventually called the day of Pentecost, is often referred to as the birthday of the Christian Church.

We began by supposing. Now suppose the early Christian we have been listening to leaves us with our thoughts. We have learned something of what it was like to experience the different stages of Jesus' presence. We know that by the very nature of things we cannot experience that immediate physical presence. We cannot row a boat with him, walk with him, eat with him. Neither can we experience the second mode of his presence among them, those encounters between his resurrection and the ascension. Even the disciples themselves knew that the ascension signalled a withdrawal.

How then can we experience the presence of Jesus in our lives? How can we know Jesus Christ as distinct from knowing information about him?

Knowing Jesus Christ

How does one encounter the living presence of Jesus Christ? The first response is that men and women have encountered the living presence of Jesus in any place, at any time, in any circumstance. When other Christians tell us of their encounter or when we read of the encounters of men and women in other times it becomes quite obvious that there is no time, no situation, no place which Our Lord cannot use: Levi was in his office, Moses was out on the farm, Paul was riding to a committee meeting, Mary was drawing water, Francis met a leper, Julian was desperately ill, Teresa of Avila dreamt of a great castle, C.S. Lewis was on a bus going to the zoo, Augustine was in a garden, Jean Vanier was on the bridge of an aircraft carrier.

In the Gospel of Thomas, never included in the New Testament, Jesus says, "Cleave the wood and I am there. Turn a stone and you start a wing." Its a beautiful way of expressing the truth that there is no place or time which cannot become the encounter between Jesus and our human experience.

So for each of us the encounter will be different, yet for all of us there are certain tried and tested ways. They are like great gates which countless people over the centuries have found helpful in the search for God. These gates, if we want to use them, serve to place us at times where Christ passes by.

The first gate is that of Christian community, of relationships. You and I would never have met on this page were it not for the fact that someone at some time called each of us in Jesus' name. At some stage in both of our lives someone has told each of us something about him, showed us some symbol of him, shared with us one of his stories, taught us a simple prayer. Who knows when that was or who that was or where it was. But in each of us some seed was sown. It may be that recently a friend, someone you love, or a business colleague, has triggered in you an urge to search for what Jesus Christ might mean in your life. If that is true it is important to realize that not only do we search for Jesus Christ but also he searches for us. The relationship is a two-way street.

The second great gate to the city of our spirit is God's Word. Four people have given us four vivid portraits of Jesus. We call them gospels. No other writing in the world has been subjected to so much criticism, ridicule, analysis, derision, as these gospels. Yet after two thousand years here they are, as true and as magnificent as ever. They show no sign of losing their mysterious power to draw men and women of every conceivable kind to Jesus Christ.

The third great gate is sacrament. On the night he was betrayed Jesus took some bread, broke it, and gave it to his disciples. He said, "This is my body." Then he took the cup of wine, gave it to them, and said, "This is my blood." The Bible says that we are to continue this act until Jesus comes again, and Christians believe that every time we do, Jesus is present among us. Simple? Mysterious? True? Absolutely.

The fourth gate is the Holy Spirit. In everyone's journey in search of Our Lord there are moments of great doubt, and also moments of great certainty. In the latter moments, or periods, doubts fade away and we know with joyful certainty that Jesus is Lord. His very existence saves us from the hell of meaninglessness that life can sometimes become. Such moments are breakthroughs: they are like oases in the desert, like burning bushes, or a sudden stream of pure water. They can be like light breaking into a dark place. Just as the disciples were behind locked doors and suddenly Jesus was among them, so we can feel locked in by many aspects of life only to find that Jesus is present with us. Such moments cannot be organized or programmed, they are the gift of God. All we can do is to allow ourselves to remain open to the possibility of such encounters.

That last sentence is as good a description as any of the fifth great gate, the gate of prayer. Most of us have strange ideas about prayer. We are all certain that there must be some right or expert or official way to pray: there simply is not. Ask the great saints and mystics, and you will find that even they flounder and despair about prayer at times. We all think that other people know more about prayer and pray better than we do, but it simply is not true. We all think that prayer is always words, perhaps, ideally, flowing Elizabethan prose! It simply is not. At its deepest level prayer is learning to place ourselves where the Christ may pass. Prayer is keeping a rendezvous with Our Lord even if it is only fifteen seconds while a traffic light changes!

Prayer is living perfectly normally while remaining open to the possibility that an encounter with Our Lord can take place in any circumstance. Compared to Our Lord, the Scarlet Pimpernel knows nothing about disguises!

Called for What?

Let's suppose that reading these pages has been a help. Let's suppose, too, that reading them is only part of a lot of searching you have been doing recently. Perhaps you have been talking to someone or have been invited into a group; perhaps you have tried worshipping again after many years. Perhaps you have tried moments of tentative prayer or have read one of the four gospels. Perhaps all this is completely new for you!

Suppose that you have become aware of something happening that you can't quite describe: someone or something is trying to get in touch with your deepest self. You may not be quite sure whether somebody is trying to get in touch with you, or you are trying to get in touch with somebody! If so, you have already joined a vast number of men and women of every type and age and ability and race and language. They have felt what you are feeling. In more cases than you could number they have found that Jesus Christ is the person and the power and the reality they have been looking for, and who, believe it or not, has also been looking for them.

Jesus himself is really talking about this very experience whenever he speaks of the kingdom of heaven or the kingdom of God. Remember how we were saying that he would tell endless stories about people who had lost something or somebody, and they would go looking until they found what was missing. That is precisely what we are doing. We have a sense of something missing, a gap or a void in our lives. We may have material things without number; in fact, life may be very good. However, there is sometimes a void at the heart of things, and we very badly need to find what will fill it. Not a day goes by but men and women somewhere discover that Jesus Christ can fill that emptiness, that he is the reality lost from their lives. Usually when this happens there is a real sense of discovery, a sense of joy and peace and new meaning. That is why Jesus always finishes his stories of finding lost things by telling us of a celebration, a party.

Another bit of supposing. Suppose Jesus Christ has become real for you. You have always been totally real for him! That is another way of saying Jesus loves us, something many Christians feel is a bit sentimental and gushy. Suppose you have come to the point of realizing that his call is to you: you have accepted him as Lord of your life. Then the question is: What has Jesus called you for?

The simple answer is that Jesus calls each of us to serve him for the rest of our lives. What does serving Jesus mean? Does it mean being "religious," doing religious things, meeting religious people, ending up in religious places? The honest answer is that it should involve us in such things, but we need to be crystal clear that all of the above are only means to a far more important end. If we become Christian we will certainly want to worship God in some community. We will want to seek his presence in prayer, however groping and halting. We will want to study the things that have been written about him. We will find ourselves feeling comfortable with some people — not all — who also believe in him. But all of these things are for something else beyond themselves.

What Our Lord wants is for us to give the full potential of our humanity to him. We don't necessarily have to change what we are doing; we may choose to, or we may choose to change some things. Most people find that they continue doing what they are doing and being who they are, only there is a new depth and meaning and satisfaction. Of course deep and costly changes in our lives may occur. Something we have always taken for granted as absolutely indispensable to our happiness may, when seen through the eyes of Jesus, look amazingly pointless and rather stupid! Maybe the way we conduct some of our relationships has to change. We may realize the selfishness and exploitation of others in our deepest relationships. We may come to realize the need to change the way we use our affluence.

There may be astonishing consequences to allowing Jesus

to become Lord of our lives. We will be opening our eyes for the first time to the realization that he is not only Lord of our life but he is Lord of all life. Suddenly, Jesus, whom we used to think of as a long-ago figure in history, or a religious figure in a stained glass window, or a pleasant sentimental memory of our childhood — this same Jesus becomes Lord of the way we think and the way we decide and act about everything, whether it be our personal affairs, our community's attitudes, our country's politics, or our relationship with the environment.

Maybe it is easier now to see why people like Paul and John could never be content with showing us Jesus on a small scale. They tried to get us to see that the events which took place on that small stage can encompass a person's whole life and, indeed, the whole of human experience.

Now go and write the rest of this book: you are the only person who can finish it. There are four gospels in the New Testament, but in Christian experience there are really five. The fifth is yours. You have a co-author: his name is Jesus.

Between Us Again

The day I took this manuscript to the post office I met Saint John again. I had just picked up the fat brown envelope and was leaving the car when suddenly he was there beside me. He smiled and said, "How can we get you people to realize that there are no walls between your world and ours. In fact, I shouldn't even use that expression. There is no such thing as our world and your world. All creation is His."

I was still startled so I said a stupid "Whose?" "The Lord's" said the saint, with a trace of exasperation. "The Lord Jesus, or, as I call him in my book, the Word. Creation is all His. Actually another word I use that might help is — 'mansions.' I recall Jesus saying that in the Father's house are many mansions. Does that help you to understand, even though at your stage you cannot live in them all?" "Can you?" I asked. "Yes," he said, "it's one of the many advantages of what you call death."

"Do you know when I first began to suspect the existence of this freedom to move among the many mansions of creation?" he asked. "It was when Peter and I got to the tomb that morning. We ran all the way. Mary had just burst in and told us, and Peter and I didn't even wait to ask her a question. We just started running. I could hear Peter panting and gasping behind me until he fell away behind. I was much younger, you remember."

"Why didn't you go in?" I asked. "Well," he said, "just think of the situation I was in. It was only when I got there that I was suddenly aware of the enormity of what Mary had said. I realized that no matter what I was going to see in there I was going to be terrified. I was either going to see Jesus' body or I wasn't. If I did, Mary was wrong and everything was over. If I didn't, then either something ghastly had happened to

Jesus' body, or Mary was correct and the world was never going to be the same again. So no wonder I hesitated about going in. Wouldn't you?''

"Yes," I said, "I must admit I would have hesitated too. But what do you mean by saying the world would never be the same?'' "Well," said the saint, "what do you think?'' There was just a hint of impatience in his tone. "Everything was indeed changed, wasn't it? After all, you are one example of that. Here you are two thousand years later with His cross on your forehead and this manuscript about Him in your hand." I instinctively put my hand to my forehead. "Oh, don't worry," Saint John said, "it doesn't actually show. However we can always see it once you have been baptized. It always stays there even if you forget or don't care about it in the least. You can't ever hide it from us, or from Him."

"But," I prompted, "you did go in." "Yes," he said, "but only when Peter arrived. He barged right past me. Peter was like that, but it was wonderful to have him there at that moment. I went in after him.''

For a long time there was silence. I looked sideways at the saint. I knew he was back in the tomb again trying to accustom his eyes to the darkness. Eventually he turned to me as if he were coming back from a long journey. Very quietly and deliberately he said, "Only the cloths were there. I will always remember that — only the cloths. It was the way they were lying that told me everything. They were there just as if the body had dissolved and had left to re-form itself somewhere else.''

Again there was a long pause, as if the saint didn't know what else to say. "Did you and Peter say anything?'' I asked. "No," he said, "at least nothing I can recall. I don't think I recalled anything in my book, did I?'' "No," I assured him, "you didn't.''

We both paused. I had a sudden feeling that after all these centuries of living with the reality he was still awestruck by what had happened. "Yes!" he said, suddenly and vehemently, "Of course I am." I was confused. "You are what?'' I asked. "Awestruck," he said. "That's what you were thinking, isn't it? Even after twenty centuries I'm awestruck. But, you know'' — he leaned toward me — ''what awes me even more than what happened then is what goes on happening.'' ''What do you mean?'' I asked. ''Well,'' he said, ''look at you mailing this manuscript. Why did you write it unless you are awestruck too? You've just tried to do something as I did centuries ago. You've gone looking for his body but you found him to be alive. That's what has always been so awe-inspiring. It's not just that Jesus rose, but that he is always rising and always will be.''

The saint's eyes were sparkling. ''You see,'' he said, ''that's what you and I and everyone who has ever gone to that tomb has in common. We have Him in common — His love and His spirit and His life. That's why He came. Don't you see? He came that you and I and everyone who finds Him might have life.''

I didn't know what to say. For a moment I thought the saint was leaving because it seemed to me that he was becoming less visible. Then I realized that my eyes were misted a little because he had moved me so deeply. To cover my confusion I said a stupid thing. I lifted the manuscript and said, ''Have I left out a great deal?'' ''Oh, yes,'' he said, ''of course you have. But then so did I, so does everybody who tries to write about Jesus. No one will ever tell it all: it's far too wonderful and mysterious and glorious.''

He looked at me a long time in silence and I had a sudden, terrible feeling that he was trying to think of a kindly way of telling me not to mail the manuscript; I wondered if he were waiting for me to offer not to. With every passing minute I began to realize a score of good reasons why I shouldn't. But Saint John put out his hand. He pointed towards the manuscript in my lap and said very gently, ''Go and mail it anyway. Jesus accepts all our gifts however unworthy they may be.'' For a moment my eyes looked down, instinctively following his hand. When I lifted my eyes again, he was gone.